What People Are Saying About

All I Ever Really Needed to Know About Life, I Learned From a Rubber Band

Written with profound wisdom, this amazing book is an extraordinarily empowering resource that will guide you towards authentic empowerment and personal awakening. It is a must read for anyone who wants to move beyond life's struggles and into a life lived with inner truth and joy from the inside out.

—Barbara Rose, Ph.D.,
Author of *Stop Being the String Along: A Relationship Guide to Being THE ONE* and *Know Yourself: A Woman's Guide to Wholeness, Radiance & Supreme Confidence*

Lisa Hepner's analogy of the rubber band is absolutely profound. This book takes the reader on a journey through the drama of human life, touching on the multitude of life experiences, situations and circumstances that all of us face. How refreshing to have such an empowering book that literally shows the reader how to enhance the human journey using proven spiritual principles and philosophy. This is a must read.

—Dr. Angelo Pizelo,
Founder and Director of Emerson Theological Institute

Lisa's book, *All I Ever Really Needed to Know About Life, I Learned From a Rubber Band* is full of helpful advice and pragmatic tools on how to live a more fulfilling life. Her unique combination of humor and wisdom is very refreshing!

—Chris Michaels,
Author of *Your Soul's Assignment*

Lisa has written a very important book. It is so important to *not* be in denial and to realize that once we see what is going on in our lives and feel the pain and then let go that it can be a very positive experience. In the letting go we create a higher vibration. Sweeping challenges under the rug will never help us. We must face our fears and then change our vibration to what we *can* do instead of what we can't do. I highly recommend Lisa's book.

—Michele Blood,
Best Selling author *How to Become A Magnet To Hollywood Success*, and producer and host of MPowerTV.com

The problem with spiritual principles is we take them way too seriously. Spirituality is supposed to be fun. Lisa, in this light-hearted, witty book, turns spiritual principles on their head, transforming them into something we actually might enjoy pursuing.

—Pam Grout,
Author of *Living Big, Art and Soul* and *God Doesn't Have Bad Hair Days*

Lisa Hepner is a young woman who has been there and back. Her experiences with life and the wisdom she has gained from those trials have molded a beautiful young Spirit who shares her tragedies and triumphs so succinctly in her book, *All I Ever Really Needed to Know About Life, I Learned From a Rubber Band*. Read this book and you will be gently directed to an inspired path of peace and joy.

—Bill O'Hearn,
Author of four inspirational books including, *From the Heart of a Child*, and *Other Lessons to Live By*

In *All I Ever Really Needed to Know About Life, I Learned From a Rubber Band,* Lisa writes with a wisdom beyond her years. She has the gift of making life simple and connects to her readers by her willingness to be vulnerable. She shares personal stories that let you know she has walked your path and graduated to a higher state of peace and serenity. When I read the table of contents, I knew I wanted to buy this book! After reviewing it, I definitely want several copies. Lisa writes to your experience while sharing her experiences. A masterful story-teller she paints a picture with words of a journey of our own mental hell on earth and gives practical tools for breaking free of our negative, degrading thinking. The rubber band is the teacher and Lisa the narrator. It is practical, wise and holds the answers to releasing from resistance.

—Perry A~,
Speaker and Author of *People Are Just Desserts*

All I Ever Really Needed to Know About Life, I Learned From a Rubber Band

by

Lisa Hepner

All I Ever Really Needed to Know About Life, I Learned From a Rubber Band

Copyright ©2006 by Lisa Hepner

All rights reserved, including the right to reproduce this book or any portion thereof in any form. No part of this publication may be reproduced, stored in a retrieval system or transmitted in any form or by any means, electronic, mechanical, recording, photocopying or otherwise, without the expressed written permission of the author.

Published by Peaceful Earth, LLC
www.peacefulearth.com
Beaverton, Oregon

Cover Design by Wes Wait, *www.weswaitdesign.com*
Author Photo by Frank DiMarco, *www.dimarcoimages.com*
Rubber Band Photo, *www.photos.com*

ISBN 13: 978-0-9715845-2-5
ISBN 10: 0-9715845-2-4

www.lessonsfromarubberband.com

For my mom, Jane and
my husband, Michael.
Thank you for showering me with love.

For Mike Gerdes;
Thank you for gently nudging me
to find my own inner voice.

CONTENTS

Introduction ... i

PART ONE: How to Quit Shoving Your Rubber Band under the Rug

Chapter 1:	Land of Denial	3
Chapter 2:	Labeling—Good or Bad?	5
Chapter 3:	My Experience of Acceptance	9
Chapter 4:	Your Experience of Acceptance	13
Chapter 5:	If I Deny It, It'll Go Away	15
Chapter 6:	The I-Don't-Know-How Epidemic	19
Chapter 7:	Addictions: A Form of Denial	21
Chapter 8:	Drama Queen	27
Chapter 9:	Sitting with Your Pain	33
Chapter 10:	I'm Pissed Off!	39
Chapter 11:	But You Make Me So Angry	45
Chapter 12:	I'm Afraid	49
Chapter 13:	You Are Not Your Rubber Band	55
Chapter 14:	The Imposter	59
Chapter 15:	Skeletons in the Closet	67

PART TWO: How to Stop Cutting off the Flow of Life with Your Rubber Band

Chapter 16:	Resist and Twist	75
Chapter 17:	Releasing What Doesn't Serve You	79
Chapter 18:	Release for Peace	83
Chapter 19:	Meditation for Releasing	89
Chapter 20:	The Path of Least Resistance	93
Chapter 21:	Hard Work or Resistance?	95
Chapter 22:	Decisions, Decisions	99
Chapter 23:	Listening to That Still, Small Voice	101

Chapter 24:	Attached to Outcome	105
Chapter 25:	Experiencing Joy	109
Chapter 26:	Passive Peace	113
Chapter 27:	Imposing Your Will on Someone Else	117

PART THREE: How to Stop Hurting Yourself with Your Rubber Band

Chapter 28:	Living from the Inside Out	123
Chapter 29:	Reactive or Responsive?	129
Chapter 30:	Take a Deep Breath!	137
Chapter 31:	Meditation	139
Chapter 32:	Affirmative Prayer	143
Chapter 33:	Affirmation Basics	153
Chapter 34:	Loving Yourself	157
Chapter 35:	Loving Your Body	163
Chapter 36:	Relationships as Mirrors	167
Chapter 37:	Dormant Dreams	171
Chapter 38:	The Most Natural Thing	175
Chapter 39:	Passion	179
Chapter 40:	Right Before the Miracle	183
Chapter 41:	Fear of Failure and Rejection	187
Chapter 42:	Worry over Finances	189
Chapter 43:	Fear of Death	195
Chapter 44:	Using Words as Weapons	199
Chapter 45:	Seeking Expert Advice	205
Chapter 46:	Playing the Martyr	211
Chapter 47:	Gratitude	215

PART FOUR: How to Stop Hurting Others with Your Rubber Band

Chapter 48:	Realizing our Unity From a Bottle of Bubbles	221
Chapter 49:	Honoring All Beliefs	223
Chapter 50:	Love Is My Religion	227

Chapter 51:	Us vs. Them	231
Chapter 52:	Transparency	235
Chapter 53:	Send Someone Love	237
Chapter 54:	Seek to Understand	241
Chapter 55:	Victims and Perpetrators	249
Chapter 56:	"FORE"giveness	255
Chapter 57:	Grudges	261
Chapter 58:	Listening as a Loving Act	265
Chapter 59:	Acknowledging Others	267
Chapter 60:	Cooperation Instead of Competition	269
Chapter 61:	Our Effect on Others	273
Chapter 62:	See Peace	277

Epilogue 281

Acknowledgments 287

About the Author 289

INTRODUCTION

Jane gets out of bed in the morning, tired from a restless night of sleep. Instead of sugar plums filling her head, she was plagued with incessant mind chatter about an upcoming work project, her child's destructive behavior, her spouse's lack of intimacy, and her looming credit card bills.

Jane is late for work again, cursing the traffic and blaming her spouse for the delay. Once at work, she is instantly bombarded with dozens of insignificant things to do. Her supervisor is on a rampage and takes everything out on her because he doesn't know how to deal with the stress of upcoming deadlines and his own dysfunctional patterns. Not knowing how to handle her supervisor, Jane, too, snaps at others around her.

There is so much bickering, gossip, and backstabbing among her co-workers that Jane feels as if she's stuck in a soap opera. The work day finally ends, but she takes work home with her because she has pressing deadlines.

Now she has to think about dinner. She fights the crowd of shoppers at the grocery store and becomes irate at the person in front of her in the express lane with twenty items.

As she pulls up in the driveway of her home, she notices what appears to be a drunken man yelling at a woman next door. She turns her head, pretends she doesn't see anything, and goes inside to throw something together for dinner.

When she realizes that the dinner she envisioned isn't going to happen because everyone is on a different schedule, she cleans up and packs leftovers. The phone rings. It's a debt collector. She hangs up the phone stressed out.

Jane catches a glimpse of her wedding photo on the mantle and wonders where all those happy days went. She finally seeks solace in her favorite chair, alone in front of the television, looking for a way to vegetate. But she can't get comfortable because her shoulders and neck ache from stress.

She turns on the news only to hear about the war in Iraq, the feud over gay marriage, and the increasing violence on the streets. She then looks at the clock and wonders why her adolescent daughter isn't home yet. Worried, she goes to the liquor cabinet and pours a stiff drink, hoping to take the pain away. She then slips into a depression, wondering if it will ever end—wondering if she will ever experience peace in her life, if her relationships will ever just flow, and if the people of the world will ever be able to peacefully co-exist.

Does this story sound familiar? It is the life story of the average Jane or Joe. Statistics show that approximately 75 percent of Americans are plagued with stress, anxiety, or depression. Almost everyone suffers from some sort of addiction—alcohol, cigarettes, recreational drugs, prescription drugs, food, sex. The divorce rate is the highest it's ever been. Suicide rates are rising. Gang violence has increased.

Introduction

Clearly, most of us are not experiencing peace in our daily lives or in our relationships.

So what is the key to ending all this suffering? I have explored this topic in great detail and have found a solution using a simple *tool* that can help us achieve peace in our lives, our relationships, and the world.

But before I go into that, I must explain that I originally intended to name this book *All I Ever Really Needed to Know About* Peace, *I Learned From a Rubber Band*; yet I decided *not* to use the word "peace" in the title because over the years I have found that it has many different connotations and brings up mixed emotions.

Often, when people hear the word "peace," they don't understand how it relates to them or why it is important. The word "peace" brings up issues of duality (i.e., for or against). It is most often defined as the "opposite of war." And it is often an intangible notion. People don't understand what peace really is, why they need it, or how to achieve it.

Yet if you talk about life and how to live the best life possible—how to live a life of abundance, joy, health, harmony—people see the importance.

Especially if you create a real-life example like the one about Jane, previously, and you see yourself living this life—then it really becomes important. If you see yourself in the beginning story, then you definitely know how wonderful it would be to experience peace in your life.

Part of my mission in this book is to redefine peace as a way of being—a way of living. That way, the word applies to all.

If I were to give you tools to experience a life of harmonious and loving relationships, abundance, creativity, health, and inner stillness, would you like that? What if I were to give you tools to create peace in your life? Would you like that?

Peace is synonymous with experiencing loving relationships, harmony, vitality, abundance, creativity, joy, and inner calmness.

Gandhi said it beautifully when he said, "Peace, to be real, must be unaffected by outer circumstances." What if we could get to an inner place where we would experience calmness, joy, and love no matter what was going on in our life situations? Would that be helpful?

What if the following story could be *your* story?

Jane gets out of bed feeling refreshed from a peaceful night's sleep. She feels gratitude for a new day to experience new things. She is excited to go to work because she loves her job and has many ideas to share.

Jane is late for work because of the traffic, but she uses this time alone in her car to practice her deep breathing and listen to uplifting, inspirational music. When she gets to work she is excited to see all her co-workers; she thinks of them as one big family. Her boss snaps at her because of an impending deadline, but she doesn't take it personally. She knows he is going through some personal struggles at home as well as experiencing the pressure of deadlines at work. She allows his negative comments to just bounce off her.

Jane goes into a meeting in a spirit of joy and finds that it is contagious. Ideas are shared, input is gathered, and the meeting is constructive and fun. Everyone works together for the benefit of the team. Everyone's personal gifts and talents are brought to the table and acknowledged.

When the workday ends, Jane is excited about getting home and preparing a family meal. She loves to cook and finds it another outlet for her creativity. And dinner is a family event. Everyone savors the flavors and aroma of a home-cooked meal.

At the dinner table, everyone talks about his or her day and shares any insights gained or obstacles encountered. It is a positive, uplifting conversation in which all family members are encouraged to express who they are, without judgment or condemnation.

As the children go their separate ways after dinner, Jane has some time alone with her husband. They tickle one another on the couch and lovingly give each other a short massage. They light a candle and relax in one another's arms.

The phone rings. It is a nonprofit organization calling to thank Jane for her recent generous donation. She smiles, knowing she is really making a difference.

Jane decides to take a nice hot bath and then curl up on the couch with a good book. The family cat snuggles with her by the fire. She falls asleep on the couch, peaceful and totally relaxed. Her husband lovingly wakes her up with a kiss, and the two head to bed. Jane sleeps peacefully and wakes up rejuvenated, thankful for another day.

Does this story sound familiar? If not, it *can* be your life experience.

This book will show you *how* to have the above as your experience by using a simple tool that I discovered one day while experiencing a bout of the infamous writer's block.

My attention, that day, was everywhere except on the article I was supposed to be writing. I wanted to present the topic—the spiritual principles of inner peace and world peace—in a simple, easy-to-understand way.

Because I learn primarily through entertainment, I like to come up with unique ways to deliver and present material. I love telling stories, both my own and others. I believe that when we are engaged in a story, we can learn valuable lessons without feeling like we're learning.

I also believe that we inherently *know* most of these spiritual principles, and that it's just a matter of finding a tool or unique perspective to help us *remember* these principles.

I normally take pride in my ability to come up with creative, entertaining ways to explain concepts, but this time I was stumped.

Introduction

When I'm not feeling very resourceful I usually take a break and get away from the project. I often have to just let an idea percolate for a while.

But this time, instead of leaving my computer, I propped my feet up on my desk, leaned back in the chair, grabbed a rubber band from my desk, and began to fiddle with it as I scanned the collection of books on my shelf.

I noticed Robert Fulghum's book, *All I Really Need to Know I Learned in Kindergarten*, and remembered how much I enjoyed its simple premise.

Then I thought to myself, "What if all we needed to know about peace we could learn from a rubber band?"

I laughed at first, but then my mind began to run with the topic.

Now, after almost a year of *toying* with the concept, I am absolutely convinced that all we need to know about life, we can indeed learn from a rubber band.

If you happen to have a rubber band handy, I encourage you to grab it and play with it for a moment.

Let's say that the rubber band represents our life experiences: our situations, circumstances, and events. The rubber band is a symbol of form and all that happens in the world of form.

The rubber band is neutral. It just "is." In and of itself, it can't hurt us and it can't hurt others. But what we *do* with the rubber band matters.

Predominately, we do one of four things with our life experiences (our rubber bands):

1. We avoid or ignore our experiences until they accumulate into a big mess.

2. We twist and contort our experiences in an effort to make something happen, and in that process we actually cut off the flow of life.

3. We use our experiences or circumstances to hurt ourselves.

4. We use our experiences or circumstances to hurt others

First, many of us live in denial. We ignore our experiences by shoving them under the rug. That's like taking a rubber band and hiding it under the rug.

What would happen if we continued to do this with our life experiences? We'd end up with a big ball of rubber bands all tangled together under the rug. Can you picture that tangled mess?

How many of you have tried to clean up such a mess? It's virtually impossible to untangle all those rubber bands once they've accumulated to that extent.

Some of us deny (avoid or ignore) our life experiences because we think they define us. We somehow think that we *are* our rubber band.

Introduction

Second, many of us take our circumstances, situations, or experiences and twist them, contort them, and try to make something happen.

Trying to make something happen would be like taking your rubber band and twisting it a couple of times around your wrist.

Please do *not* try this with an actual rubber band. Why? Because you'd cut off the circulation to your hand.

When we try to make things happen, or resist our life circumstances or experiences, it's as if we are taking that rubber band and twisting it around our wrists. We literally cut off the flow of life.

Life wants to work; life wants to flow. By trying to make something happen or by resisting something that is happening, we stop that flow.

Third, many of us allow our experiences, circumstances, or situations to hurt us. We hurt ourselves by the way we think or react to our life experiences.

We play the victim, we reprimand ourselves, we feel guilty, we feel worthless, we belittle ourselves, we judge, and more. That's right—we use our experiences to hurt ourselves. It's as if we took the rubber band and *snapped* ourselves with it.

If you have a rubber band handy, I invite you to put it around your wrist and snap yourself with it. Ouch! That hurts, doesn't it?

Would most of us really continue to do this to ourselves over and over? I don't think so. And yet this is what we really *are* doing any time we belittle ourselves, degrade ourselves, neglect ourselves, or overreact to a situation. Any time we feel guilty, angry, sad, or hopeless, or any time we hold a grudge, we are literally hurting ourselves. We are metaphorically snapping ourselves with a rubber band.

And finally, the fourth thing many of us do with our life experiences is direct our anger or pain outward toward others. That's like taking a rubber band and shooting it at someone else.

Note: Do *not* try this stunt at home. This stunt should only be performed by a trained professional and in a controlled environment where no one can get hurt. Shooting a rubber band at someone is very dangerous. People have literally lost an eye because of a rubber band.

What normally happens when we shoot someone with a rubber band? We get a rubber band shot right back at us. If we get angry at others, they usually get defensive or angry right back at us. Lashing out at others in anger solves nothing. As Gandhi said, "An eye for an eye leaves the whole world blind."

Most of us may not even realize that we're hurting others with our life experiences. I don't think any of us would willingly shoot our loved ones or co-workers with a rubber band.

Yet if we belittle others, if we judge them, if we yell at them or degrade them, we are metaphorically shooting a rubber band at them and hurting them.

So how do we get to the point where we don't constrict the flow of life? Where we don't ignore our life circumstances? Where we don't hurt ourselves or others with our experiences? Well, that is the main focus of this book.

The book is divided into four parts based on the four things we do with our life experiences (our rubber bands).

Part one is about how we can get to the point where we are able to deal with our life experiences without ignoring them or shoving them under the rug. It's about how we move from denial to acceptance, from suppression to expression.

Part two is about how we can get to the point where we stop resisting our life experience, detach ourselves from specific outcomes, and instead allow things to unfold.

Part three is about how we can avoid hurting ourselves with our life experiences by living from the inside out, loving ourselves, and accepting ourselves as the wonderful beings that we are.

Part four focuses on how we can get to the point where we do *not* use our circumstances and experiences to hurt others. It is about honoring all beliefs, creating and maintaining peaceful relationships, and expanding our compassion outward to the world.

As you continue to work with the analogy of the rubber band, you will find that this simple, everyday item really has much to teach us about experiencing peace in our lives, our relationships, and the world.

And, at the end of the book you will be invited to take the rubber band challenge, which is a way to remember these principles *and* explain them to others.

PART ONE:

How to Quit Shoving your Rubber Band under the Rug

Chapter 1
Land of Denial

Let's face it—we live in a land of denial. Even as you read this statement you may deny the full truth of it.

But take a look around. Nearly everyone currently suffers from some sort of an addiction. And basically, addictions are sedatives or cover-ups for our pain. They are a form of denial.

We deny our pain by using a substance or engaging in a behavior that makes us feel better temporarily. Many of us, unable to face our current condition or situation, turn to recreational drugs, alcohol, cigarettes, sex, food, prescription drugs, or unhealthy relationships in hopes of making the pain go away.

Instead of dealing with the pain or anger, we suppress it with substances or destructive behaviors. Most of us have become experts at *suppressing* our emotions (denying them), but we are ill-equipped at *expressing* them in a healthy way.

So the question is; why do we deny our emotions, situations, or experiences? Why do we try to shove them under the rug?

We live in a land of denial for one of the four reasons listed on the next page:

1. We deny our experiences because we have labeled them as "bad" and we don't want to deal with them.

2. We deny our experiences because we think that denying them will make them disappear.

3. We deny our experiences because we flat out don't know *how* to deal with them constructively. Many of us don't know how to deal with our pain so we numb it with a substance or a destructive behavior.

4. We deny our experiences because we think we *are* the experience. We think we *are* our past, our feelings of rejection, or our fear.

Living in denial is equivalent to taking our rubber bands and shoving them under the rug. Remember what happens when we do this? We end up with a big mess that is difficult to untangle at that point.

In the next chapters, we will explore how we can move from denial to acceptance, and from suppression to healthful expression of our emotions. Only then can we find our way out of the land of denial.

Chapter 2
Labeling—Good or Bad?

Many of us deny our experiences because we perceive them as bad. After all, it's easy to accept the good things that happen in life, right? But it's difficult to accept the bad things, so we often ignore or deny them.

One day while exploring this topic, I came across a joke on the Internet that shows what happens when we label things good or bad. *(Please know that telling this story does not mean I endorse hunting).*

Once upon a time in Africa, a king and his loyal squire were out hunting for food. The squire was known for his "Pollyanna" attitude. He always looked at the bright side of everything.

No matter what happened, the squire would always say, "Ah, this is good." Even if something really bad happened, the squire would still say, "Ah, this is good!"

One day the squire was helping the king load his gun when it accidentally went off and shot off the king's finger. As the squire grabbed a bandage to stop the bleeding, he said, "Ah, this is good."

The king was outraged. "How can this be good? I lost my finger. This is terrible!" The king was so mad that he sentenced the squire to five years in prison.

Then one day while the king was out hunting alone, a group of cannibals captured him and took him to their village. The king was in a dire situation. He knew that he would soon become dinner for the tribesmen. But this group happened to be very superstitious, and one of them noticed that the king didn't have a finger. To them, he was flawed, so they immediately let him go.

The king then realized that his squire was right: it was a good thing that he had lost his finger. Had he not lost his finger, he would have been eaten by the cannibals. So then he started feeling really bad that he put the squire in prison.

The king went to visit the squire in prison and shared the story with him, saying that the squire was right all along, that it was a good thing he had lost his finger. Then the king admitted, "I feel terrible. It was a bad thing for me to put you in prison." But the squire smiled and said, "Ah, this is good."

The king was shocked. "How can you think this was good? You've been imprisoned for almost five years of your life. How is that good?"

The squire smiled and said, "If I had not been in prison, I would have been out hunting with you."

One reason we deny our emotions is because we label them. Again, how many of us are eager to deny the emotions we deem bad, emotions like pain, anger, and stress? And how many of us openly accept those emotions that we deem good?

Labeling—Good or Bad

Eastern traditions stress the importance of being unattached to outcome, both good and bad. Yet our human minds are attached to labels and duality.

But, how often have you judged something as really bad and then later realized that it really was a good thing? Have you ever felt devastated when a boyfriend or girlfriend left you? You thought it was the worst thing possible. But then later on you met this great guy or gal and realized that had you not been through that supposedly bad breakup, you would never have met this wonderful person.

On the flip side, I'm sure there have been many times when we thought something was really good and it ended up being bad. Maybe at the time, smoking felt really good but ended up being really bad when it led to breathing complications.

Also, it's interesting to note that what you think is good may be bad to someone else, or vice versa. It all depends on perspective. And it all comes from our minds.

Two people can experience the exact same situation, and one can think it is bad and the other can think it is good. For example, let's say it is pouring rain outside. One person might look out the window and say, "Oh no, it's raining," meaning they perceive the rain as bad. Whereas another person in the room might look out that same window at the pouring rain and say: "Wow, I love the rain!" or "How refreshing the rain is!"

Really, there is no "good" or "bad"; everything is simply what it is. It is our thoughts, feelings, or reactions that make things either good or bad.

Instead of labeling something as good or bad, accept it by saying, "It is what it is." I think you will be amazed at how your acceptance will change your outlook on life.

In the next two chapters, I will share my experience of accepting something I perceived as bad, and a powerful exercise to help *you* accept any situation you perceive as bad.

Chapter 3
My Experience of Acceptance

In 2001, I quit my job in medicine to pursue my passion for writing and creating. (You'll get the full story in part three).

I had been diligently working on Web site marketing for Peaceful Earth for a couple of years, working on such things as building a brand name, learning about search engine submission and auto responders, and building subscriber lists.

I had also been working on products for the Web site like Internet movies, E-cards, books, E-books, and E-courses. I had spent lots of money on marketing programs and educational programs teaching me how to sell products online. Yet no matter what I did, I could not make money from the Web site.

At one time, I even requested donations through a friend's non-profit organization. That didn't work, so I continued to send out announcements of specials in which I bundled things together and offered them for a very low price. Yet I still wasn't making enough money to even cover the monthly Web hosting costs.

Then one day, I got a bill from my Web host provider for around $500.00. If I didn't pay it, my Internet movies and my Web sites would be down.

This was like death to me. After all, the sites had been my baby for the last couple of years.

If my sites were down, I would be out of business. I wouldn't be able to get speaking gigs, sell books, or advertise. I wasn't sure how I would continue with anything.

At this point, I had already sold everything of value to obtain money for rent and bills. Now I wasn't sure if I would be able to pay rent or anything.

I was devastated. I was in pain for a week. I didn't answer my phone, leave my apartment, or do anything. I felt as if my life was over.

But then an interesting thing happened. Toward the end of the week, I finally surrendered. I accepted that my sites would go down. I accepted that I might have to change my situation, perhaps move in with my parents or figure out something else. I accepted that everything I had could be gone.

This is when the miracle happened.

Despite the possibility of losing everything, I experienced an inner calm. I had the thought, "Even if I lose everything, I still have *me*." I realized that I could re-create—that I still had creativity and passion to start over and create new things.

I got excited thinking about getting back to basics and getting back to my writing. I had been working on several screenplays and a couple of books before I started devoting all my energy to the Internet. I was excited. I felt that I could concentrate on my writing. I released my Web attachment and decided to get back into screenwriting.

Once I fully accepted my situation and was at peace with it, another miracle happened.

I went to my mailbox about a week after this devastating experience and found an order for some of my products. Because I was a week late in filling the order, I wanted to contact the customer about the delay.

Interestingly, the person who had placed the order included an E-mail address on the order form even though the form didn't ask for it, so I decided to E-mail him and apologize for the delay.

The customer E-mailed back, saying not to worry about the delay and that he had ordered the product as a gift. I noticed that his E-mail signature included a URL: *www.screenplaymastery.com*. Of course this caught my attention.

I looked at his site and discovered that he's a script consultant in Hollywood. He helps screenwriters sell their movies.

I E-mailed him again and told him of the "coincidence." Since then we've gotten to know each other. He's been up to Portland, where I live, and I was able to attend his workshop for free by helping him with handouts and other things.

Also, I got some one-on-one consulting from him while I drove him to his hotel and had lunch with him. From attending his weekend workshop, I came up with a new screenplay, a romantic comedy called *Twin Flames*, which I completed this year. I had never tried writing a romantic comedy before, but I had a blast.

Also, I was able to work out the financial details with the hosting company. As it turned out, they had overbilled me, and therefore they refunded the money. But I ended up finding a less expensive host anyway.

This experience had felt like death to me while it was happening. I felt as if everything I had worked on over the last few years had been taken out from under me and that my life was over. Now I realize that the experience was a new beginning.

So this bad experience was a blessing in disguise once I was able to accept it and receive the *true* blessing. It ended up being one of the best experiences in my life because it helped me clarify my values and passions, and got me back to my true love—writing and creating stories.

Chapter 4
Your Experience of Acceptance

I know we all have had experiences that we thought were so bad at the time and later realized were a blessing. Remembering this fact helps me get through times when I think something bad is happening to me.

I wrote down my previous experience on a piece of paper and titled it "My Experience of Acceptance." I keep it in my desk drawer to remind me that something that seemed really bad ended up working out, or being better, in the long run.

If I feel as if something bad is happening, I take the paper out of the drawer and read it. Then I think to myself, "I thought this situation was really bad at the time, and it ended up working out; this will too."

I encourage you right now to think of an experience in your life that you thought was really bad. Maybe it was a divorce that felt like the end of the world, maybe you lost an important job, maybe you lost money and didn't know what you were going to do next. Whatever the experience, bring it to mind now.

Then think about the good that came out of that situation. For example, maybe the divorce that felt devastating at the time forced you to attend a support group where you met the love of your life. Or maybe losing that job gave you time to focus on starting your own business or pursuing a passion. Or maybe that illness forced you to re-evaluate your priorities and spend more time with your family.

Whatever it is, I encourage you to write the experience down on a piece of paper. You can title it "My Experience of Acceptance," if you like. Then keep it in your desk drawer or somewhere close to you.

Anytime you go through a situation that seems really bad, take the paper out and read it. This will help you to remember that the previous experience you thought was so bad ended up working out for the better, so you can conclude that this experience will, too.

If we continue to think of experiences as bad, we continue to resist them—and thus our growth stagnates, and we prevent the miracles from unfolding. We cut off the flow of life.

The key is to accept whatever situation or experience is in your life and *know* that it is working out as it should, even though it may not look or feel that way at the moment.

Remember: Instead of labeling things as good or bad, just allow them to be as they are. Know that terms like good and bad are relative.

Chapter 5
If I Deny It, It'll Go Away

Many people deny their circumstance or experience because they think if they ignore it, it will go away. Yet it only gets bigger or more difficult.

I know this because I have lived in the land of denial for most of my life. I lived in constant denial of my true emotions. My emotions were too painful to deal with so I'd look for an escape route. Unfortunately, those routes weren't really escapes from the pain but detours that prolonged it and eventually made it worse.

In my adolescent years, I was pretty messed up. My sense of self-worth was very low, and yet I was in denial about it.

In high school, I equated sex with love and felt that if I had sex with someone, I could get him to love me. I used sex as a cover-up (or a denial) for my true feelings of low self-worth.

In high school, in college, and even after college, I lived in denial about my romantic relationships. I kept attracting and getting involved with emotionally unavailable men or men who treated me poorly. (In retrospect, I was the one who *allowed* them to treat me poorly because of my feelings of unworthiness, which we'll discuss in more detail in part three).

In my denial I asked myself questions that perpetuated me being the victim, questions such as "Why do I keep getting involved with this type of man?" or "Why do I keep attracting this type of person?" Poor me.

Again, instead of admitting that I had anything to do with this pattern and instead of looking at my feelings of unworthiness that attracted unhealthy relationships, I lived in denial, thinking that I was the poor, innocent victim.

What happens when we continue to deny our emotions? We keep attracting the same situations. When we don't deal with our circumstances, situations, experiences, or emotions, they continue to show up, or get worse.

For example, in my situation I would run from one relationship to another only to experience the same problem over and over again. And each time, I would fall into thinking like a victim: "Why do I attract such a person?"

It wasn't until I worked on my feelings of low self-worth and accepted the fact that I did not value myself highly enough that I could begin to heal those feelings.

Once I started feeling, honoring and knowing my true value, I would ultimately attract a relationship that reflected it. And I did. (More about this in part two).

As you continue to read my history, I invite you to ask yourself if you have ever denied any of your emotions—sadness, anger, stress, fear, low self-worth—through some sort of addiction or destructive behavior.

If I Deny It, It'll Go Away

Again, if you have, you are not alone. But also know that when we deny things, we make them bigger.

Acceptance is the road to healing and inner peace. Can you learn to accept the emotion that is underneath the destructive behavior or addiction?

If you can, the destructive behavior or addiction will fade away. More about this in the next chapters.

Chapter 6

The I-Don't-Know-How Epidemic

Let's take a look at what else happens when we deny our emotions. Most often, our emotions eventually express themselves in the form of violence toward ourselves or others.

People who suppress their anger (or other emotions) are like walking time bombs that can explode (violence toward others) or implode (violence toward oneself) at any time or as a result of any seemingly trivial event.

In many cases, the denial or suppression of pain drives people to take their own lives. Many of us deny our relationship issues until we end up in divorce court with no chance of reconciliation. Many of us deny a physical symptom until we have a life-threatening condition we can no longer ignore. Many of us deny our financial situations until we end up in bankruptcy court. Many of us even deny our addictions, thus making it difficult to effect any positive, lasting changes.

We need to recognize an important distinction: The problem is *not* the expression of anger but the expression of anger in a way that is harmful to oneself or others. The problem is *not* the expression of fear but the expression of fear in a way that is hurtful to us or others.

We must be able to accept and express our true feelings in productive ways that don't hurt anyone.

Yet, again, most of us don't know *how* to do this. Most of us have become experts at covering up our emotions through some sort of addiction.

Chapter 7
Addictions: A Form of Denial

In high school, instead of dealing with my pain of feeling unworthy, I would try to mask it with something—alcohol, cigarettes, sex, or some other destructive behavior or substance.

I used to deny my emotions by trying to drink them away. I'll never forget one horrendous night when I took a bottle of Tequila into my room and drank 14 shots back to back. I spent the whole night puking into my trash can. I could have died from alcohol poisoning. I only weighed about 100 pounds at the time. To this day, I can't smell Tequila without getting a sick feeling.

Alcohol was the sedative I used to ease my pain, or so I thought. Later I realized that drinking my sorrows away was a form of denial. But alcohol wasn't the only way I lived in denial.

If I was stressed or anxious, I'd turn to cigarettes. I used to be a heavy smoker. I started smoking at age 13. I'd quit off and on, but any time a stressful situation came into my life, I'd end up smoking again.

In high school, I also snorted a substance called Rush that was equivalent to paint fumes in a bottle. Looking back, I realize that I did this because I felt so awful about myself and wanted so much to be accepted. And, unfortunately, the people I was hanging out with were snorting glue, drinking, and having sex, so I felt that I had to do what they were doing in order to be accepted.

I'm honestly surprised I lived through my adolescent years. I remember snorting Rush one day and feeling as if my head was going to explode. I felt as if I was in a vacuum—I lost my hearing, and the veins in my forehead pulsated as if they were about to burst. Looking back, I realize that I could have died.

I also could have died or killed someone every time I drank and got behind the wheel of a car.

The reason I mention all this about my past is to show you that if you deny your emotions through an addiction or destructive behavior, you are *not* alone.

The most common way we deal with our pain is through addictions.

It's hard to find actual statistics on addictions because there are so many different types: recreational drugs, prescription drugs, alcohol, food, sex, cigarettes. Not to mention the many emotions that people are addicted to: unworthiness, fear, drama, sadness. Most people nowadays suffer from some sort of an addiction.

And all addictions are a form of denial. For example, maybe you're addicted to sex to cover up your feeling of unworthiness. Maybe you're addicted to alcohol to cover up pain from feeling unloved or rejected.

Most addiction counselors agree that no one with an addiction can be helped unless they admit the problem. The alcoholic who denies he's an alcoholic doesn't have a very good chance of fixing the problem.

I would go a step further and say that once you resolve the underlying emotion beneath the addiction instead of denying it, the addiction will go away.

For example, I mentioned earlier that I used to smoke cigarettes. I started with flavored Cloves at age 13, and then switched to regular cigarettes. During high school and college, I was smoking a pack a day. I tried everything to quit—the gum, the patch, cold turkey, subliminal tapes. Some methods worked, but only temporarily.

Then I went to a hypnosis seminar and heard that if you smoke, you want to die. That really hit home with me. I didn't think I wanted to die.

In this seminar, I participated in a hypnotic experience in which I saw myself dying from cigarettes. After that, I didn't smoke. I quit cold turkey, and every time I saw a cigarette, I associated it with death.

This worked for a couple of years. But then, during a stressful event, I went back to smoking. I find it interesting how long it took me to quit and yet how easy it was to start up again. Before I knew it, I was smoking again.

Then one day, I remembered what the presenter at the seminar said: "If you smoke cigarettes, you want to die." Again, I didn't think I wanted to die. But at the time I started smoking again, my life was a constant struggle with challenges at many levels—relationships, finances, dreams, success.

When I thought about it more deeply, maybe I did want to die.

As soon as I associated smoking with wanting to die, I quit again because I wanted to live. I practiced being in the moment and living joyously. I had a new outlook on my projects and some new direction.

Once I had a zest for life, I naturally didn't want to smoke. I wanted to go outside and play or go to the beach or eat healthful food instead. My joy for life and wanting to live conquered my addiction to cigarettes.

In other words, I wanted to *not* smoke, more than I wanted to smoke. Living a smoke-free life was more appealing than smoking.

Whereas, previous times when I tried to quit smoking, I was only quitting because I knew I should quit, but I didn't really *want* to.

Once I looked at the underlying reason for my smoking—my wanting to die—and realized that I really did want to live, my addiction to cigarettes went away.

The same theory held true for my addiction to unhealthy relationships. As I mentioned earlier, for most of my life I was addicted to unhealthy relationships with men who were emotionally unavailable or who would end up treating me poorly.

The reason I say I was addicted to this type of relationship is because it was a recurring pattern, and any act that you do habitually is an addiction.

My addiction to unhealthy relationships was a denial of my true feelings of low self-worth. Because I didn't feel worthy of love, I would subconsciously

Addictions: A Form of Denial

seek relationships that would *prove* my unworthiness; I would attract partners who would treat me the way I felt about myself.

The only way I could stop getting involved in unhealthy relationships was to accept my feelings of low self-worth and claim my true worth.

Once I admitted that I felt unworthy and really started looking at that feeling and honoring it and accepting it, I slowly started gaining self-worth. (In part two, I'll give a detailed example of how I released this destructive pattern.)

When I knew my worth and that I deserved a loving relationship, the addiction to unhealthy relationships was no longer there. I no longer attracted men who treated me poorly. My feelings of self-love allowed me to open myself up to a healthy, loving, supportive relationship.

When we look at the emotions underlying our addictions and work at them from that level, the addictions naturally fade away.

If you are addicted to any substance or behavior, ask yourself, "What am I denying through my addiction?" Or, "What is the emotion I'm trying to cover up through this addiction?"

Then bring your consciousness into that feeling and you will free yourself from your addiction.

Chapter 8

Drama Queen

Do you know someone, maybe very intimately, that seems to always have drama in his/her life? Once one thing is settled, something else pops up. There's always something!

Some people are addicted to drama. Without their *story*, they believe they are nothing. Their lives are emotional roller coasters, going up and down. When they're up, they are really up and living large, and when they're down, they're really in the dumps.

I used to be addicted to drama. Yes, I was a drama addict! And by drama, I mean intense highs and intense lows. Everything was so dramatic! It was like theatre.

In fact, at the time, monks or others that seemed to be non-reactionary and peaceful seemed boring! For me, being middle ground and non-reactionary seemed like death.

For the longest time, I didn't want to experience inner peace because I felt like if I gave up the drama, I would also have to give up the intense highs that were also part of the experience.

I had an attachment to drama. The highs were so high that I wasn't willing to give them up to *not* experience the lows, even though the lows were really low.

Yet, as with any addiction, there comes a breaking point. After constant struggling in my relationships and finances, I decided I had enough! I just wanted the struggle to stop. I wanted the lows to end.

I was reading a book, *Healing with the Angels*, by Doreen Virtue, Ph.D. about summoning your angels and I decided I needed help.

Anyway, I was desperate. I was tired of struggling. So I did an exercise where I just asked a question and let my angels (or Higher Self or intuition) provide the answer.

Here is what happened: (My questions are printed in regular print and the answers from my inner voice are in italics).

ME: It seems I'm always struggling. Getting into a panic about how I will pay rent; how I will pay my bills.

INTUITION: *Yes, this seems to be a pattern. Do you like the drama of struggling?*

ME: Hmm. Yes, there is drama in struggling. It's never boring…Okay, maybe I do create my own drama, but I don't want to live this way anymore.

INTUITION: *Keep claiming that. Refuse to live month to month. Accept your abundance.*

ME: How?

INTUITION: *Know you are worthy of abundance. You desire money to sustain you in doing what you love. Claim your abundance. Know your worth.*

ME: But what should I do?

INTUITION: You don't have to do anything other than what you are doing. Just continue what you are doing with your writing. Be active, don't let the circumstances of life paralyze you and put you into a victim mode so that you can't do anything...

This was interesting because my paralyzing worry had been a recurring pattern in my life experience. I'd get so sucked into fear and worry at times, that I couldn't do anything, often for days.

But why would I be addicted to feeling down and out and struggling?

I remember a saying from *A Course in Miracles* that said something like, whenever you're feeling sad, depressed or angry, you must believe that the particular emotion "buys" you something.

What would being down and out buy me? What would struggling buy me?

Well, my drama bought me sympathy. When I was down in the dumps my friends would remind me of how wonderful I am!

My drama bought me acknowledgement. When I was experiencing a high from a success I would let people know about it and they would give me praise. My drama bought me appreciation, and it bought me sympathy as well. No wonder I was addicted to it!

I mentioned earlier that all my previous relationships were very dramatic with intense highs and really intense lows. Unfortunately, the lows were really bad. Some would call these types of relationships "love/hate relationships" because they oscillated between two extremes. However, this is not true love because true love has no opposite.

In fact, I thought a healthy, stable relationship seemed boring. And I know that many women feel this way as well. Thus the phrase, "nice guys finish last."

My husband is one of the nicest men you'll ever meet. We have a wonderful relationship that just flows. We rarely argue although we do have our disagreements. Our relationship isn't a love/hate relationship. Our relationship is loving and supportive. There's a sense of just flowing with the current.

Once I gave up my addiction to drama, first by recognizing it, I was able to create circumstances that didn't involve drama.

Once I gave up my addiction to drama, I didn't have to search for relationships that brought drama.

If you are addicted to drama, ask yourself what the drama buys you? Allow the answer to come up without forcing it. Or you can ask yourself, "How has this drama served you?" Again, allow the answer to unfold.

Once you receive an answer, ask yourself, "How you can get that experience in other ways?" For example, if your answer was that your drama serves you because it makes you feel appreciated, how can you feel appreciated in other ways?

Or, if your answer was that you are addicted to drama because you feel that a part of you will be

Drama Queen

lost if you give up the intense highs, ask yourself how it would feel to give up the intense lows? And, what if you could find a middle ground and still experience great joy?

Just realizing that I was addicted to drama helped me move from drama to middle ground. And I can tell you that I haven't lost myself, but gained a deeper awareness of my true self. And I experience a *consistent* joy in my life.

Chapter 9
Sitting with Your Pain

The next few chapters will help you transform pain, anger and fear to peace instead of denying it.

Many of us deny our pain because we don't want to be seen as wimpy. We deny our anger because it's often socially unacceptable to be angry. We deny our fear because it's important to be perceived as strong. We deny our needs because we are afraid of being judged.

We use our addictions to try to cover up our pain, anger or fear. And, when we don't deal with our pain, it is equivalent to shoving our rubber bands under the rug. When we deny our experiences or shove them under the rug, they only get bigger.

If you asked people going through a painful time to just sit with their pain, they'd most likely be unable to do it. Most likely, they would try to deny the pain or try to mask it with something.

Recently, after one of my public-speaking engagements, a woman came up to me and said she was depressed. She wanted to know what to do. I told her it was okay to sit with her pain. I told her she needed to honor what she was feeling in the moment.

Now, I know at first this may seem like absurd advice. But her struggle, her internal conflict, stemmed from her belief that she had to deny her depression. She felt that it wasn't okay to be depressed. Her internal conflict was expressed by her two beliefs: "I'm depressed" and "It's *not* okay to be depressed."

Ultimately, I explained to her that she is the embodiment of peace and that by allowing herself to feel whatever she feels in the moment, no matter how painful, she will unveil that peace at the core of her being.

I can tell you from experience that it is very powerful and transforming to just sit with your pain and not do anything to fix it or cover it up.

Remember the great alchemists who tried to change base metal to gold? Well, when you sit with your pain, you can succeed where the alchemists failed and transform your pain into peace.

Underneath all that pain and turmoil, there is a place of peace. Ancient religions talk about moving "beyond your mind" to that place of peace. There is a center of perfection within you. You may not be able to see it or experience it while you are feeling pain, but it is there. Taking a moment to sit with your pain can be one of the most transformative tools available to you.

We can see how sitting with our pain works when we look at the grieving process after the death of a loved one. Most of us wouldn't tell a wife who has just buried her husband of twenty years to stop crying and get over it. We would allow her to experience grief and know that it was natural. The wife would create space for the pain and allow herself to grieve. Then, naturally, when the time was right, the sun would shine again and she would carry on.

I think the reason most people don't want to sit with their pain is that they think it will consume them. They believe they will never come out of it.

Some people who experience severe pain believe that they will never escape it; they think the only way they can experience peace is by taking their own lives. Others think that the only way they can handle their pain is to inflict it on others.

People who inflict pain on themselves and others are what Eckhart Tolle would term "unconscious." In his book *The Power of Now*, he talks about "going into the pain and transmuting it." There is a difference between consciously sitting with your pain and unconsciously being consumed by it. (We'll explore this concept later in the chapters "You Are *Not* Your Rubber Band" and "The Imposter.")

Again, it is transformative to sit with your pain or whatever emotion you're feeling at the time and not do anything to cover it up or fix it. It's important to bring your consciousness into the situation.

I used to love to call people and tell them about my pain. And through their sympathy I would somehow feel a little better. When they acknowledged that I was a victim, my pain was temporarily eased.

But one time when I was experiencing financial devastation after quitting my job to pursue my passion, instead of covering it up or reaching out to others, I just sat with the pain. I invited it to dinner, so to speak. I really dived right into it.

I had a pity party. I got out my CD player and my Cat Stephens CD. I grabbed a box of tissues, and

I listened to "Oh, baby, baby, it's a wild world. It's hard to get by just upon a smile." I kept hitting repeat, repeat, repeat . . . And I cried and cried and cried.

Because my financial problem was so painful and so scary, I sat with my pain for a few days. It didn't get better after just fifteen minutes. I cried and cried off and on for three days, and fully experienced my pain. Then something happened.

My whole energy shifted. It was as if I had lived my worst nightmare. I had been to the depths of my suffering, where it seemed as if everything in the material world had faded away. But I was still here.

I had a sense that I was okay, that there was an energy that would re-create, that was eternal, and that wasn't based on where I lived or what I did. It was an epiphany, like seeing a rainbow after the storm.

Prayer and meditation are powerful tools for affirming the peace beyond the pain, but when we are in the heart of the pain, it may be hard to pray or meditate, so we must go directly into that pain.

Sometimes our experiences are so painful that meditation or prayer just don't seem to work. And that's okay. Sometimes it's necessary to go into the pain, to allow ourselves to experience it and transmute it.

Most of us have been programmed to *not* go into the pain. We cover it up, we avoid it, we mask it, or we anesthetize it through addiction. But we can gain tremendous power from being fully present with the pain.

Sitting with Your Pain

What we will begin to notice if we can do this, is that at the very core of that pain is peace.

Next time you are feeling pain, tell yourself that it is okay to feel it. Go within and really experience the pain. Sit with it.

Play that sappy song that brings on the tears. Be present with your pain, and you will become the alchemist who transmutes pain into peace.

It is important to learn to honor whatever we are feeling in the moment. It is important to bring our consciousness into whatever we are feeling.

Chapter 10

~~I'm Pissed Off!~~

We only need to turn on the television to see the results of anger—Bombs going off everywhere; people shooting one another, stealing from one another, and inflicting pain on one another. Or we hear about people who inflicted their pain and anger on themselves through drug overdoses or suicide.

Again, the problem is *not* the anger itself but the unhealthy expression of anger toward ourselves or others.

We often deny our emotions because we think we *are* our emotions. For example, if I'm really angry, maybe I think that makes me an angry person. I don't want to be seen as an angry person, so I deny my anger.

Instead of denying our anger, we really need to start talking about how we can deal with it constructively.

Can it be safe to admit that we're angry? And how do we express our anger? It is often socially unacceptable to be angry.

Some of the techniques that I've read about for diffusing anger are simple, such as taking deep breaths. (I'll talk about breathing and meditation in depth in part three.)

But when you're in the heat of anger, does deep breathing really work? Can you really stop and take some deep breaths when all you feel is anger or rage inside?

I know that when I'm in the heat of anger, I have a hard time taking a deep breath. When my emotions set in, I don't think clearly. I act from an unconscious level or my "Imposter" has taken over. (We'll explore the concept of the Imposter next.)

In other words, my pain or anger has become my identity and completely consumed me. So, what can you do at this point?

I find that it helps first to admit that I'm angry. I don't deny my feelings of anger. I allow myself to be angry. Before, I would feel angry and tell myself over and over that I wasn't angry. But I really was angry, which led to even more internal conflict.

Now, I allow myself to have a temper tantrum if that's what I'm feeling. How many of us have seen kids throw a temper tantrum, get it all out of their system, and then go their merry way a few minutes later?

Of course it isn't socially acceptable for an adult to throw a temper tantrum at work, and it's definitely not appropriate to hurt someone else with your anger, physically or emotionally. When I throw a temper tantrum, I do so in the comfort of my own home or car, where no one else can hear me.

The point is that we've got to be able to release our anger in a productive way—whether it's stomping our feet, hitting or screaming into a pillow, or just rolling on the bed and ranting. It's important to accept our feelings in the moment.

I'm Pissed Off!

Now I may get some negative feedback from this comment, but I believe boxing has helped me deal with my anger.

You may think that boxing is contradictory to peace, but it has been a channel for me to release my anger. I'm a recreational boxer, meaning that I work on the heavy bag and speed bag, and occasionally I spar while wearing full protective gear.

It feels great to pound on a heavy bag when I'm angry. The physical release feels good. Boxing has worked for me. The point is, it's important to find something that works for you.

What else can you do to release your anger? Think about this now. Write down some things you can do to release your anger.

Now write down some things you could do to *prevent* getting angry (e.g., talking about your true feelings instead of bottling them up inside, working out, etc.). Then start doing these things.

There are really two components to dealing with anger: (1) how to prevent anger from building up to the point that you eventually explode, and (2) how to release it when you're feeling really angry.

Again, physical exercise helps me release anger or stress. Instead of letting the emotion build, I take some action right away. Sometimes listening to music helps me diffuse my anger. My husband likes to go for a race around the track in a go-cart when he feels his anger building up. It helps him release that extra adrenaline. You need to determine what works for you.

But what happens when you're actually raging? What can you do?

Anger directed toward another person isn't appropriate, but you've still got to do something with that anger. Consider taking a "time out." Tell someone that you're feeling angry and that you need to remove yourself from the situation for a while to cool down.

My husband and I have worked out a system in advance: if we're really angry at one another, one of us yells "time out" and goes to the bedroom to hit a pillow or yell into a pillow. We have agreed to remain apart for at least 15 minutes to allow ourselves to cool off. (Ironically, since we've put this plan into place, neither of us has had to use it, but it is there when and if an anger bout should occur.)

My friend Lynda attended a seminar and learned an interesting exercise to release anger. It involved inflatable balloons. You blow up a balloon and use a Sharpie pen to write on it the names of the people or situations you are angry with. Then you express your anger at those people or situations and stomp all over the balloons. Imagine how good this would feel!

Or, you could go for a jog, lift weights, or do whatever helps you to release that anger. Then, when you are in a calm state of mind, you can re-engage in that conversation or situation. Remember: you don't want to deny the situation; you want to accept it and deal with it.

The important thing is to figure out a game plan before anger strikes. Then use it when you're angry. If you wait until you're angry, your game plan will be created from a place of anger and therefore may not be constructive.

Another way of looking at anger is to define it as "pain expressed." If you think about it, all anger results from being in pain about something and not having a way to deal with it—feeling out of control or helpless—or from being in pain about something and having it build and build until it finally explodes.

Beneath *all* anger is a deep-rooted pain. The trick is to discover what the pain is about and how you can transmute it.

So next time you're angry, ask yourself, "What pain am I feeling?" Maybe you're angry at your spouse and you realize that the pain you're feeling is the pain of not being heard.

If you can do whatever it is that you have determined works for you to release your anger, then you can later talk about the pain of not being heard in your relationship. Then the two of you can work together at finding solutions to how you can feel that you're being heard. (By the way, in part four, I will talk about violence stemming from the feeling of not being heard.)

In conclusion, know that it is okay to be angry. It is important to honor whatever you are feeling in the moment. Plan ways to release stress, pain, and anger so that they don't accumulate. Think of ways to deal with your anger once the emotion takes over.

And remember that behind your anger is some sort of pain. If you can figure out what the pain is, and dissolve it, the anger will also dissipate.

Chapter 11
But You Make Me So Angry

Some of us deal with our anger by blaming it on someone else. This is also a form of denial because we are not taking responsibility for our own anger and instead placing the blame on others.

I'd invite you to answer this question: Do you own your anger? Or do you blame someone else for *making* you angry? Is it always *their* fault?

Most people, if they even admit they are angry, will say that it is because someone *made* them angry. Most of us say things such as "You make me so angry" or "It was John's fault. If he hadn't done such and such, I wouldn't have gotten angry. He just presses all my buttons!"

The thing is it shouldn't matter what other people do; it is up to *you* how you respond. If you were completely centered in peace, no one should be able to affect you. Gandhi said, "Peace to be real must be unaffected by outside circumstances."

We cannot be responsible for other people's actions or reactions, but we are responsible for how we respond. To say that someone makes you angry or makes you a certain way is a denial of your personal power.

There is a story about Buddha, paraphrased on the next page, that illustrates what it would be like to *not* let yourself be affected by someone else:

All I Ever Really Needed to Know About Life

There was a man who made it his life mission to try to irritate Buddha. He saw how peaceful and spiritual Buddha was and took it upon himself to try to get a reaction or rise out of Buddha. He would follow Buddha around and curse and call him names, yet the Buddha would remain unresponsive and peaceful.

The man just knew that Buddha would one day reach his boiling point and respond with anger or frustration, so the man continued insulting Buddha with a vengeance. He cursed, he yelled, he made gestures, he did everything in his power to get a reaction from Buddha, and yet Buddha did nothing.

The man spent a couple of years just trying to get a reaction from Buddha, but to his surprise Buddha always remained calm.

One day the man couldn't take it anymore and decided to ask Buddha how he could remain so calm in the face of all those negative comments and anger directed at him.

The man turned to Buddha and said, "All these years I've been cursing you, yelling at you, and trying to hurt you, and yet you have remained calm. How are you able to do that?"

Buddha smiled and asked the man a question. "If someone gave you a gift that you declined to accept, who would the gift belong to?"

The man thought about it and said, "If someone gave me a gift that I declined to accept, I guess the gift would belong to the person who gave the gift."

Buddha smiled and said, "Ah yes. So if I refuse to accept your abuse, who does it belong to?"

The man paused and frowned. All of the cursing and name calling and everything had basically bounced off Buddha and had been given back to him. He was the one carrying all the anger and frustration inside of him.

What if we could all become mini Buddhas so that whatever someone said or did, it wouldn't affect us and would instead bounce right off of us?

Other people can say or do whatever they choose, and we must learn how to *not* be affected by it. We are responsible for our own response. We can *choose* how we respond to any person, situation, or experience. We can respond with peace and love, or we can react in anger. The choice is ours.

If someone is lashing out at you in anger, and you're tempted to lash back, remind yourself that all anger is "pain expressed." Ask yourself, "What if this angry person is going through something very difficult and experiencing a great deal of pain inside that I don't know about?"

Would this make it easier for you to allow his/her angry remarks to just bounce right off you? Or would it allow you to see him/her through different eyes, so that you could help him/her deal with the underlying pain? (We'll discuss this issue in more detail in part four, Understanding Someone Else's Point of View.)

Own your feelings instead of placing blame on someone else. Remember that you choose how you respond to any situation.

Practice allowing other people's comments or emotions to just bounce right off of you and not affect you.

Realize that you *choose* how you respond to any situation. You don't have to take on anyone's anger or pain.

Chapter 12
I'm Afraid

We have seen that when we deny our anger it often implodes or explodes. The same is true of our fears. When we deny them, they often get bigger or they paralyze us, preventing us from living our greatest life experiences.

Any time we deny our feelings, we are taking our situations (our rubber bands) and shoving them under the rug. And, again, remember what happens when we do this?

Have you ever heard of or read the book *Feel the Fear and Do It Anyway* by Susan Jeffers? Well, the title itself is a gem of wisdom. Just as there is transformative power in sitting with your pain, there is transformative power in confronting your fears.

I have had two major fears in my life—fear of public speaking and fear of death. And I'm in good company: these are the two most common fears almost everyone has. Yet these fears had limited me in many ways.

I have always wanted to be a writer, and I have always known that in order to be a successful writer I would have to be a successful marketer. I knew that at some point or another I would have to get up in front of a group and sell my idea or sell my book. I would have to speak in public.

So I knew that if I really wanted to be a successful writer, I would have to get over my fear of public speaking.

I decided to confront my fear head on by joining Toastmasters. Many people think Toastmasters helps you *eliminate* your fear of public speaking; I believe it helps you channel that fear.

See, I still get nervous before every speaking engagement, but now I'm able to channel that fear into energy. The more I confronted my fear by just getting up there to speak, the less hold that fear had on me. Again, the fear hasn't gone away completely; I've just learned to accept it and channel it.

The point is that instead of denying the fear, I worked with it. Instead of ignoring it, I found ways to channel it.

Public speaking, which was one of my greatest fears, is now part of what I do for a living. The fear has not gone away, but it doesn't paralyze me; it doesn't prevent me from following my dreams.

It also helps to confront your fears in a loving, supportive environment which Toastmasters provides.

My other big fear was of death. To me, death seemed like an unfair punishment. It seemed as if it unwillingly claimed innocent lives and caused nothing but pain.

I think my fear of death had been heightened by being in the medical field as well. Every day I worked with patients who were on their death beds or dealing with life-threatening illnesses.

I'm Afraid

I also think that some of the prayers we learn as children, can add to that fear. Remember the prayer, "Now I lay me down to sleep, I pray the Lord my soul to keep. If I should die before I wake, I pray the Lord my soul to take?" That's enough to make you afraid of death!

Plus, my well-meaning mother (not placing any blame) frequently used to say things like, "If I die while on this vacation, you know where the valuables are." So I found myself as an adult, constantly fearful of death.

I had heard that in Eastern traditions it is common to contemplate death in order to free yourself from your mind or body. At first I thought this was morbid. Contemplating your own death? Yikes. Eckhart Tolle in the *Power of Now* refers to this as "dying before you die."

So one night I contemplated dying. My chest immediately tightened as I thought about it. Yet, I surrendered to the feeling of dying. Once I surrendered, my body felt light and I felt free.

Then an interesting thing happened. I noticed some fears coming up: Who would take over my work on the Web site? Who would finish the screenplays or books I was working on? This was a huge *a-ha* moment for me because I realized the root of my fear of dying.

I was afraid of dying because I was afraid of not completing all the things I wanted to do. After I realized this underlying fear, I somehow felt peace knowing that the books would still get written, the movies would still be made, and life would still go on.

Really, from a Higher perspective, everything would go on as it should.

This exercise also brought me another realization: when I died, it wouldn't be *me* who died because there was more to *me* than my physical body.

When I did this exercise I felt light like I was pure energy. I realized I wasn't my body or my mind. I sensed that a part of what I thought was *me* would live on forever. It was a very powerful experience.

I'm not saying you should contemplate death if that doesn't feel right for you. The point I am making is that when you accept your fears, the fears lose their power over you.

Now I admit, sometimes that old fear of death creeps its way back into my life experience, and usually it's because of ego stuff like "I don't want to die because I have too much to do" or "I don't want to leave my husband."

But then when I think about it deeply, I know that whatever needs to be done will be done and that a part of me will always live on even after my physical body has departed.

And also, by not being so afraid of death, I am able to enjoy life more fully. That is also why people who have had near-death experiences are so fully present in the moment.

So what's your biggest fear? Can you dive into that fear? If you can delve into your fears, you will realize that what you feared actually doesn't have

I'm Afraid

the power over you that you thought it did. You will realize that there is an eternalness and infiniteness to all of us that is greater than any of our emotions, circumstances, or situations. And even greater than our bodies.

This eternalness is what we are going to explore next.

Chapter 13
You Are Not Your Rubber Band

I mentioned earlier that part of the reason many of us shove our experiences under the rug is because we think we *are* our experiences. If I'm angry, that must mean I'm an angry person; because I don't want to admit that, I'll just ignore or suppress my anger—I'll shove it under the rug.

Or maybe I believe that I *am* my past. If I did something in the past that I thought was bad, than I might shove that under the rug and try to forget about it. Or if I'm fearful, maybe I think that means I'm a coward, and I don't want to be a coward.

But, as I mentioned earlier, when we shove things under the rug we just end up with a huge mess of stuff. When we suppress our anger, we often implode or explode. When we run away from our past, it often comes back to haunt us. When we believe we *are* our life experiences then we act like something we're not. (More on that in the next chapter "The Imposter.")

A critical step to keep ourselves from shoving our experiences under the rug is to recognize that we are *not* our life experiences.

If you have a rubber band handy, go ahead and put it around your wrist. (You can also order a special rubber band bracelet from our site at www.lessonsfromarubberband.com.)

Remember that the rubber band represents your life experiences—things that happen in the physical realm. It represents your circumstances, situations or conditions.

Now just take a look at the rubber band around your wrist. Know that the circumstances, situations, and conditions that it represents are in your life experience (you're wearing it) but they are not *you*. In other words, they are a part of your life (they are around your wrist) but they are not *you*. You know you are not your rubber band.

The key to experiencing inner peace is to get to the place where you notice your life experiences but you know that they are not *you*. Therefore you have no need to react to the situations, label them, hurt yourself with them, or hurt others with them.

So if you are not your life experiences, than who are you?

Here is what *you* are:

You are pure Spirit. You are pure love and perfection. You are creative, and you are infinite. That is the Essence of who you are. That is the Essence of every individual.

Some people call it Spirit, which means "the vital principle or animating force within living beings." I call it Essence, which means "the inherent, unchanging nature of a thing." The two are synonymous. Some also call it God, Consciousness, Presence, Being, Higher Self, etc.

Now in the rubber band example, the rubber band symbolizes your experiences and *you* symbolize your Essence. And by you I am referring to your Spirit, your Essence. But what is the difference between your Essence and your experiences?

Your experiences in life involve what happens at the level of physical form *and* how you deal with what happens or how you perceive what happens (through your thoughts, your mind).

Your Essence never changes. It is eternal. It doesn't judge. It is perfect peace. Your Essence is basically that energy that remains after your physical body has departed.

When you have a certain experience in your life, it is like the rubber band on your wrist. It is in your life experience, but it's not who you are. The rubber band (or experience) is there, but it is not you. It is external to you.

The idea is to learn to notice the rubber band and not try to hide it (shove it under the rug) or label it. You want to become the observer of your life experiences by just saying, "It is what it is."

You want to get to the point where you *know* that you are more than what is happening at the level of form, that you are not defined by your outer circumstances.

Your experiences are what happens at the level of form, your Essence is the truth of who you are beyond form.

The key is to be able to make the distinction between your experiences and your Essence. Your Essence is eternal and infinite. It is pure peace.

It is the energy that is *you*. Again, it is what is left of you after your physical body has departed. It is the creative energy of the Universe.

Below are some common terms that have been used to describe the differences between your Essence and your life experiences.

Terms for Essence	Terms for Experience
God	Ego, Mind
Higher Self	little self
Spirit	Body, Mind
Universe	Form
Infinite	Finite
Being	Imposter
Consciousness	Unconsciousness
Energy	Form
Eternal	Limited
Life	Life Situation

Note: Life and life situation are terms Eckhart Tolle uses in his book *Power of Now*.

Sometimes, as I mentioned earlier, our life experiences are so painful that we react with anger, hurt, or jealousy. At this point, our Imposter has taken over. (Eckhart Tolle uses the term "pain-body" to describe something very similar).

Either way, it is a false sense of self and is not really the truth of who you are. No "thing" (experience or situation) can ever change the truth of who you are.

Chapter 14
The Imposter

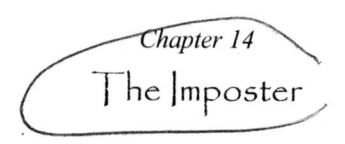

An Imposter is defined as "one who assumes an identity or title not his own for the purpose of deception."

Have you ever been so angry and done something so absurd that afterward you said to yourself, "What happened? Who was that? That wasn't me. That's so unlike me." If so, you have experienced your Imposter.

The funny thing about your Imposter is that it makes you think it's *you*. I know the Imposter and recognize it quite well because *it* had been running most my life.

Now wait a minute. Imposter? It sounds as if you're describing multiple personalities or something. Well, let's go back to the basics in order to understand this notion of an Imposter.

Going back to our Essence, *all* of us are pure Consciousness, pure Spirit, pure Energy.

If you study quantum physics or just read a little bit about it, you will discover that the energy that created the Universe is actually the same energy that makes up *you*. You are the creative energy of the Universe! Cool, huh? You are pure Essence, pure Spirit.

Basically what I am saying is that *you* are a miracle. You are wired for perfection. You are a unique expression of the Universe. You are an expression of

God. You are the Universe continually unfolding, and you have infinite potential.

But you also have this thing called your mind. And your *mind*, because of your upbringing, society, status, social climate, experiences, and so forth, has different beliefs or perceptions.

Your thoughts can make you feel limited, restricted, isolated, or separate. And that is what I call your Imposter. Your Imposter is the belief that you are separate—your belief that you are imperfect or flawed or limited in any way.

I have often said that the key to inner peace is healing our sense of separation from our Source. Our thoughts (our minds or ego) can make us believe that we are separate from our Source. Our minds can make us believe that we are separate identities. And it's those separate identities that I call our Imposters.

Basically, when you are *not* showing up as who you are—unlimited, joyous, peaceful, abundant, healthy, and perfect—then your Imposter has taken over.

Your Imposter will make you believe that you can't do something, that you aren't good enough. Your Imposter sometimes takes over in such a way that you feel you are *it*. If you are overrun by your emotions, your anger or your pain—that is your Imposter.

When you are run by your emotions, you are experiencing your Imposter. It is not your true self. Your true self is your Highest Self, your Spirit/Soul, your Essence—all that is whole, complete, abundant, joyous, peaceful, and perfect.

The Imposter

Then there's the Imposter that shows *its* nasty head sometimes. It really isn't you, even though you've created this separate identity and you believe it's you. (And sometimes it sure takes over!)

Again, your Imposter is your belief that you are separate from your Essence, your Source.

Other people have called this Imposter the "little self." Eastern traditions have labeled it the "monkey mind." It does not matter what you call *it*, as long as you know that *it* is not *you*. It's a false sense of self that you have created, but it's not *you*. It is what Tolle refers to as unconsciousness. If you are fully conscious of who you are, your emotions would not take over.

Now wait a minute, you may say, aren't you giving people free passes to avoid being responsible for their actions by saying, "It wasn't me; it was my Imposter"?

In one of Eckhart Tolle's audio series he talks about teaching consciousness to children, and about recognizing and naming the pain-body. So for example, if a child has a temper tantrum, the mom might ask the child, "Who was that monster?" Maybe the child says it was "Angry Billy." Now you have a tool to use with that child to help him notice when Angry Billy comes up. Why is this important? Because the key to getting Angry Billy under control is to notice when Angry Billy shows his little head.

The key to experiencing inner peace is to notice and recognize your Imposter (or pain-body) as a separate entity that you have created and thereby dissolve it.

Imagine what the world would be like if we all had our Imposters under control and they weren't set loose to destroy ourselves or others. Or better yet, what it would be like if we all acted from our true Essence rather than from our Imposter?

So what's the solution to taming or dissolving the Imposter? The solution is to first start noticing *it*. The next key is to realize that the Imposter is not *you*.

Once you start to notice the Imposter, you have separated yourself from *it*. Again, the key to inner peace is healing your sense of separation from your Source; by claiming that you have made a separate identity for yourself and knowing that you are not *it*, you free yourself to acknowledge the truth of who you really are.

Going back to the rubber band analogy, it's like saying you are *not* your rubber band. So while those circumstances or situations are happening in your life experience, you are *not* your circumstances or your situations.

Again, if you wear the rubber band around your wrist and the rubber band represents your situations and circumstances, you can just look down at the rubber band and say, "I see. It is what it is. I notice it. It's there. But it's not me. It's not the truth of who I am."

The fact that you notice *it* (the Imposter) means that you have given up your identification with *it*. You are no longer feeding it, you no longer give *it* any energy, and *it* therefore eventually dissolves.

The Imposter

Many of us have heard the story about two dogs fighting. One dog represents evil (anger and pain), and the other dog represents good (peace and kindness).

A student asks his master, "Which dog will win?" The master replies, "Whichever one you feed."

If you feed the Imposter, *it* gets bigger; *it* gets more energy. If you don't feed *it*, *it* loses energy and dissipates.

When you start noticing the Imposter as if you were a casual observer, then you no longer feed *it*. When you become the Imposter acting from anger, rage, or pain then you give *it* more energy.

That's not to say that you should deny the Imposter because once *it's* taken over, *it's* in full force. At that point you are behaving as your Imposter. You believe yourself to be your Imposter. So it's important to equip yourself with some of the tools previously mentioned to allow yourself to feel whatever you're feeling in the moment.

But the first step in taming your Imposter is to notice *it*. When I react defensively to something my husband says, I can stop and realize that my Imposter has taken over. Just knowing that *it* is not the truth of who I am has been very liberating.

It has also been very liberating for my husband and I to notice each other's Imposter. So for example, if I'm reactive and angry, my husband will say, "That's your Imposter." I can then notice *it*, and dissolve *it*.

When you are over run by emotions, start affirming that it is your Imposter and not the true you.

Affirm that you are pure Spirit—you are love. Notice and affirm that you have created a separate identity for yourself, and that you are not *it*—that you are *not* separate from your Source. And then start to watch your Imposter disappear.

Affirmations as a Form of Denial

I want to make an important distinction here about the word "affirm" used above. Affirmations are an expression of the ultimate Truth and should not be used as a form of denial.

If I am angry, I can recognize that *it* is my Imposter that has taken over and is angry. I can recognize that *it* is a separate identity that I have created for myself. I can also affirm that I am pure Spirit. This affirmation is the Truth.

But to affirm that I am happy and peaceful when I'm really angry is a denial. I can affirm that I am feeling very angry, and that I know there is an ultimate truth to me of peace. But to say I'm peaceful when I'm raging with anger is a denial.

I strongly believe in the power of affirmations, and we will discuss them in detail in part three, but I do not believe in using affirmations as a form of denial.

For example, if someone very close to you experienced the death of a loved one and they were in great pain, would you say to them, "You are complete happiness and peace?" No, that would be a denial of what they are experiencing. But you could affirm, "I know there is a center of peace beyond the pain you are feeling."

What if you literally don't have enough money to pay a bill and you affirmed, "I have the money to pay this bill." Would this be an affirmation or a denial? I believe it would be a form of denial. But what if you affirmed, "I know the Universe is infinite and abundant; I know that I am an expression of the Universe; and I know that while I may not be able to see abundance right now, the law of abundance is working through me to provide for me." Do you see the slight distinction?

I've seen many people use affirmations as a denial of what they are feeling, and sometimes it has done more harm than good. The key is not to deny what is going on at the level of form but to proclaim the Highest Truth.

Affirmations are a declaration of the ultimate Truth beyond our human perceptions (or experiential truths), but it is important to honor what we are feeling in the moment *and* to affirm the truth.

It is also important to start recognizing that if we feel lack, limitation, fear, pain, anger, and so forth, our Imposter has taken over. We have made a separate identity out of *it*, and we are acting from that place.

Once we begin to notice our Imposter (our Ego, Pain-body, Mind) for what *it* is, we can begin to dissolve *it*, and then we can respond from our true Essence.

In summary, once our Imposter is in full force, it's important not to deny *it*. It's important not to deny our emotions, because at this point we have literally become our Imposter (our pain-body, ego). We have become the separate entity that we have created.

But it is also important to recognize that ultimately *it* is our Imposter that is behaving this way and that there is a truth of us that is greater than anything that is going on at the level of form.

It is important to remember that we are pure Essence and that we are never separate from our Source, even though we may have created a separate identity for ourselves that we believe to be the truth of us.

We are always one with our Source (God, Buddha, Allah, Consciousness, Essence, Being), and it is our mind (the Imposter) that causes us to believe we are separate.

Our rubber band represents our life experiences, but it is not us. We are pure Essence—perfect love.

Chapter 15
Skeletons in the Closet

Before I end part one, I would like to discuss the past because many of us are currently held back by our past. We live in denial of our past.

We all have skeletons in the closet—things we did in the past that we're not proud of or that we regret. Or things that happened to us that we are ashamed of.

Or, to stay with the rubber band analogy, we all have rubber bands we've shoved under the rug or tried to hide.

We all have pain from our past. There isn't a single person in the world who has *not* experienced some kind of pain in the past.

So how do we move beyond the past so that it doesn't affect us in the present?

I know that many people, including me, have been held back by the past because we were unable to release a past event or action. Many of us allow our pasts to keep haunting us or we keep replaying our past patterns. Or many of us think we *are* our past.

Personally, I didn't like who I was or the decisions I made in the past. I hung out with the wrong crowd when I was younger. I did things that I'm not proud of. I was into drinking and smoking. I really didn't care much for myself or others. I equated sex with love. I hurt myself and others through my destructive behaviors.

When I look at my past, I often wonder who that person was and how I got to where I am today. My past has continued to plague me most of my life.

Yet I know that the past is really only alive in my memory. I am not the same person I was even five minutes ago.

My pain and suffering comes from believing that I am who I was back then or from reliving who I was back then in the present moment.

The past exists only in my mind. So does the future. The future is a projection of something that hasn't happened, and the past is only a memory of something that has happened. Neither the past nor the present define who and what I am *now* at this very moment.

What if you could envision a timeline and picture yourself standing at today's date? Then what if you could erase everything that happened before today? Well, you can!

The only place the past exists in the present moment is in your mind. Really, it's gone. It's done. It doesn't exist except in the confines of your memory. It cannot affect you unless you *allow* it to affect you in the present moment.

Some of us like to reflect on our positive past experiences, but those too are alive only in our memories. They are not here and now.

The key to escaping the bondage of our past is to acknowledge that our past is alive only in our memories, to acknowledge that the past does not exist anymore and that we have a clean slate.

However, it is important to deal with your past if it is adversely affecting your *present*. Some techniques for dealing with your past were described in previous chapters like "Sitting with Your Pain."

The way out of your pain, is through your pain. It's one thing to talk about your pain and another to move through it. I used to talk about my past to get sympathy. But that wasn't dealing with my past. It was just talking about it.

Once I really dived into my pain and my core issues of low self-worth I was able to be free from my past. And now, if I start to think about my past, I find it helpful to realize that my past is gone, and that all I have is the present moment.

In his book *The Spontaneous Fulfillment of Desire,* Deepak Chopra talks about how the molecules that compose our bodies change every six months or so. So in reality we are entirely new people every six months. Yet we continue to believe that we're held back by a past that doesn't even exist except in our minds.

Living in the past is like allowing your life to be ruled by a nightmare you had. At the time, the nightmare was so real and so scary. What if you woke up and continued to be haunted by the dream everyday? This is what many of us do with our past situations. We hold on to them and allow them to haunt us.

Now, I'm not discarding the events of the past and saying that they weren't real. If you were abused, raped, or hurt in the past, I'm not invalidating that. I'm only offering suggestions for moving beyond that pain and not allowing the past pain to control your life in the present moment.

When I say the past doesn't exist I do not mean that whatever happened didn't happen. I mean that it only has the power to hurt you in the present moment. It is alive only in your memory. And if you are hurting from any event that happened in the past, you are allowing it to affect you in the present moment.

A part of my healing was to remind myself, every time a thought came up from the past, that the past is alive only in my memory and that it currently has no power over me. Every time I remembered the hurt from a past relationship, I would affirm, "The past is alive only in my memory. It has no effect over me in the present moment. I am pure love and peace in this moment."

But what about those of us who say our past situations affect our current behavior? For example, let's say you didn't get love from your family in the past and therefore you currently try to get it anywhere you can, and you keep winding up in abusive relationships. Your past has affected your current reality, but only because you have allowed it to. Only because you think you are your past.

If you can remember who you are in the moment (your Essence)—you won't have to keep repeating the past. You can know that *you* are not your past. Your past doesn't define you unless you want it to. You don't have to be a slave to your past.

Skeletons in the Closet

Free yourself from your past by realizing the truth of who you are at this very moment. Know that you are pure Essence and peace and that nothing in the past can change that. Neither can anything in the future . . .

PART TWO:

How to Stop Cutting off the Flow of Life with Your Rubber Band

Chapter 16
Resist and Twist

There was a story I read on the Internet about a man in India who, day after day, could be seen praying at a particular wall. News spread of the man's devotion and regimented prayer at this wall.

A reporter went to India to find out more about this man's dedication and what he was praying about. The reporter saw the man praying at the wall.

"Excuse me, sir," the reporter interrupted. "May I ask you a few questions?"

The peaceful man nodded his head, and the reporter continued with her questions.

"Sir, what exactly are you doing at this wall?"

"I'm praying," the man responded.

"That's great. What are you praying for?"

"I'm praying for world peace. Peace between all people."

"Well, that's very noble," the reporter commented. "How often do you pray for world peace?"

"I come here every day and pray for world peace."

"Wow, you come here every day! And how many times a day?"

"I come to this wall to pray twice a day."

"So twice a day, every day, you pray for world peace? How long have you been doing this?"

"For fifteen years."

All I Ever Really Needed to Know About Life

The reporter was awe-stricken. "So you've been praying for world peace at this wall, every day, twice a day for fifteen years. That's amazing. What does that feel like?"

The man was silent. "Well, it feels like . . ."

The reporter anxiously awaited his response.

"It feels like I'm talking to a *brick wall!*"

How many of you have felt like you were talking to a brick wall? How many of you have felt like you were doing the same thing over and over without seeing any results?

This is what happens when we try to *make* things happen.

Staying with the rubber band analogy, what would happen if you were to twist the rubber band around your wrist? You'd cut off your circulation.

What happens when we resist our situations or try to *make* something happen? We cut off the flow of life as well.

Life wants to work. Life wants to express through us, yet often we get in the way because we're so busy trying to *make* things happen or resisting what is happening. If only we'd let go and release, life would work itself out.

I've had many experiences with resisting what is and with trying to *make* things happen. In fact, in the past I was quite proud of my ability to make things happen.

Yet I also know that when I come up against a brick wall from trying to *make* things happen, if I release and let go, then things naturally work themselves out.

Resisting something or trying to *make* something happen is the equivalent of trying to swim upstream. Yes, you can do it, but after a while it gets exhausting.

When you release, you allow the river of life to take you where it wants to go. And ultimately the Universe wants to express its greatness through you.

When we release that which doesn't serve us, we open ourselves up to a greater experience.

Chapter 17
Releasing What Doesn't Serve You

Once there was a little girl, about eight years old, who was out shopping with her mom. The little girl noticed a beautiful pearl necklace, and she begged her mom to buy it for her.

The mother looked at the price tag. Because the pearls were fake, made of plastic, they were very inexpensive.

The mother told her daughter that she'd buy the necklace for her if the girl promised to help around the house more and do more chores. The little girl agreed.

The little girl loved her necklace. She would walk by the mirror, catch herself wearing it, and stop and stare at the necklace for hours. She would constantly touch it on her neck to reassure herself that it was there.

As promised, the little girl also did many extra chores around the house. She cleaned her room, took out the trash, and helped with the dishes.

The mother and daughter had an evening bedtime ritual of reading together. Every night after a bedtime story, the mother would watch as the little girl took off her pearl necklace. The mother insisted that she *not* wear her pearls to bed for fear they would turn her neck green.

The little girl would fall asleep staring at her beautiful pearl necklace.

One night, after the bedtime story, the mother asked the little girl if she loved her. The girl reassured the mother that she loved her. She stretched out her arms as far as they could go and said, "Mommy, I love you this much!"

The mother then smiled and said, "Do you love me enough to give me your pearl necklace?"

The little girl immediately said, "Mommy, Mommy, not the pearl necklace. But I'll give you *My Little Pony*. You can braid her tail and mane."

The mother smiled and kissed her daughter goodnight. The next night after the bedtime story, the mother asked the same thing: "Do you love me enough to give me that pearl necklace?"

The little girl again offered anything but the pearls. She said, "You can have *Barbie*. I have new outfits for her and a new car for her."

The mother refused the *Barbie* and kissed the girl goodnight. This went on for a few weeks. The mother would ask the girl for the pearl necklace, and the girl would offer to give her anything but the pearl necklace!

Then one night when the mother came in for a bedtime story, the little girl was pouting and had tears in her eyes.

"What's the matter?" the mother asked.

The little girl held out her pearl necklace and said, "Here, Mommy. I love you. You can have the necklace."

Releasing What Doesn't Serve You

The mother smiled and reached into her pocket and pulled out a beautiful pearl necklace. The little girl looked at it in shock.

The mother handed the little girl the necklace and said, "These were your grandmother's pearls. They are real. I was waiting for you to give up the fake ones before I could give you the real ones."

*Author Unknown

I invite you to answer this question: What fake pearls are you holding on to that, if only you would let them go, could be replaced by the real thing?

Chapter 18
Release for Peace

How many of us cling to something that really isn't serving us? And what if we knew that, if we could just let go, the Universe would provide us with exactly what we needed?

What if, as in the previous pearl necklace story, the Universe was just waiting to give you an amazing gift but couldn't because you were holding on to something else and didn't have room to accept it?

I used to date a guy who was a busy entrepreneur. In fact, that's what I really liked about him. He was a go-getter and was working on a really big project. He was highly ambitious and had a lot of passion.

Unfortunately for me, his project took up most of his time. Yet when we were together everything just flowed and seemed very natural. I thought we were kindred spirits.

Basically I wanted to see him more than his time allowed. I was more into the relationship than he was. I thought we would be great together. I was shocked that he couldn't see that.

But I convinced myself that it was okay to get whatever time I could because after all, I was busy too.

Nonetheless, I slowly began to realize that I was more committed to the relationship than he was. We dated for several months, seeing each other on occasion. But, again, I really liked him. I saw a lot of potential.

Anyway, I stayed around, waiting for him to give me some time, and he kept pushing me away, saying he was busy. I kept convincing myself that this was okay.

Then one day I thought to myself, "Why am I staying with someone who doesn't want to be with me as much as I want to be with him?" It was as if I was settling for scraps, as if I was saying, "Okay, Universe, I'll take whatever leftovers there are, or whatever is available."

I knew by this time, from studying spirituality for over ten years, that I was worth more and that I deserved a reciprocal relationship. I knew that I should probably break off this current relationship, but part of me wanted to have one foot in the door and one foot out the door. Part of me wanted to see him whenever he was available, and to put my feelers out there to see what else was available.

I kept thinking, "If I could just be patient and hang in there, maybe he'd realize how good we could be together."

But I knew I had to release the relationship, even though I was in pain about releasing him.

Then one day as I was driving to my friend Lynda's house to talk about it, I heard an inner voice say, "This is coming up to be healed. And once it's healed, you'll never have to repeat it again."

"Hmmm. What is this that's coming up to be healed?" I wondered.

Then I realized from looking at my past that I had many relationships with men who were physically or emotionally unavailable. It was a pattern!

"What does that say about me?" I asked myself. It said that I felt like I was not worthy of having a relationship that nurtures me as much as I nurture it. I felt unworthy of a loving, supportive relationship.

I had to take another hard look at myself and claim that I was worthy of receiving love. I knew that just as I desired a loving, conscious, committed relationship, there was someone else out there who wanted exactly the same thing. I also knew that by taking a stand for what I did want, I would attract that experience into my life.

But I kept thinking to myself, "Maybe I could just stay in this current relationship until something better comes along." How many of us have thought that?

I know from my studies that nature abhors a vacuum and that I needed to create the space for a loving relationship to enter. By staying in the unhealthy relationship, I would be saying that it was okay to receive less than what I was worth.

I came up with a powerful meditation for releasing, which I will share in the following chapter. (You can use it for releasing anything—a loved one who has passed away or any situation or condition that isn't serving you.)

Anyway, once I really released this person, just a *week* later, I met Michael—a wonderful man who is passionate, creative, sensitive, talented, and totally committed to a conscious, loving relationship.

In fact, he was so committed to a loving relationship that shortly after we met, I shared with him a book I purchased a while back called *Conscious Loving* by Gay and Kathleen Hendricks. I asked him if he wanted to work through the lessons together and he said yes. Now, this would have normally sent anyone else running!

But at that point we had both determined that we wanted a loving, conscious relationship; even if we weren't going to be together, we would still like to work through our stuff so we could experience a conscious relationship.

In December 2004, we got engaged, and in October 2005, we got married in Maui. And our relationship is far greater than anything I ever even imagined.

My husband and I are so committed to creating and maintaining a conscious relationship. We are also both committed to our own individual creative expression. And I am blessed to receive this precious gift of love.

Had I not released that which was *not* serving me, I wouldn't have been open to receive that which did.

So if you're ready to receive the miracle that is just waiting for you, first you need to give up that which doesn't serve you.

You need to create an opening. Give up that fake pearl necklace and claim the real thing for yourself.

If there is anything in your life that you're ready to release, I encourage you to use the following meditation. (We'll explore the topic of meditation in detail in part three).

Chapter 19
Meditation for Releasing

This meditation is excellent for lovingly releasing someone or something. Maybe it's a dead-end job, or maybe it's financial struggle. Maybe it's the past. Maybe it's a person who needs to do other things or be other places or has physically left this earth. Maybe he or she is with someone else.

Whatever the circumstance is, it is the highest good for you to release this person or situation and to open yourself up to other possibilities.

Figure out what fake pearl necklace you're holding onto. Figure out what you'd like to release, and then do this meditation.

Go to a quiet space and get in a comfortable position. Focus on your breathing, and when you are feeling relaxed, bring this person to mind, as visually as you can.

Think of the last time you saw the person. Where were you? What was the person wearing? Can you picture his or her facial expression? Can you picture any other surroundings or details?

If it's a situation or experience you'd like to release, picture something that represents that situation. If it's your past, maybe you can picture a movie projector playing scenes from your past. If it's a situation, see if you can picture any details of the situation. If it's a condition or circumstance, picture a color, shape or object that represents that condition or circumstance.

Once you have this person, situation or condition in mind, look at it and tell it exactly how you feel.

If you are feeling pain because you love the person and he or she doesn't reciprocate that love, go ahead and express that feeling without blame or guilt, but just as a matter of fact. Tell the person how much you enjoy his or her company, how great you have felt being together, what you admire about him or her, or anything else that you would like to say before you release the person.

If it's a condition and you are feeling afraid, go ahead and mention your fear and uncertainty about the future. If it's a situation express your feelings about it. Again, state your feelings without placing blame.

Once you have declared how you feel about the person, situation or experience it is time to give thanks for this person, situation or experience. Thank this person for being in your life, for the memories you have had, for the gifts you have received.

It may be hard to thank a situation or condition in your life, but see if you can find the blessing. Maybe the illness taught you what was really important in life; maybe the job loss helped you focus your talents on a new career; maybe the situation made you a stronger person. Try to find something to give thanks for.

Once you have said all that you want to say, picture this person, situation or experience getting smaller and smaller. Picture a small version of the

Meditation for Releasing

person being cradled in the palms of your hands as if you were holding something very fragile. If it was a movie projector, you can visualize the movie projector getting so small you can hold it in the palm of your hands.

Now say any last good-byes. Say to this person, situation or condition, "I lovingly release you."

Then lovingly release the person, situation or experience by blowing a kiss to this person, situation or condition. As you blow the kiss, picture this person, situation or condition evaporating into millions of tiny golden specks of light floating everywhere. The person, situation or experience has become millions of glowing, sparkling specks of light. Affirm that you release him or her to the Universe.

As you notice all the golden specks flowing everywhere, take one tiny golden speck and place it in your heart.

Now affirm, "I release you to the Universe, and know that a part of your Essence will always be with me in my heart." Or, "I release you to the Universe, knowing that I have taken any lessons for my highest good with me."

If the person comes back to your mind once you've released him or her, know that you don't need to think about him or her anymore because he or she is permanently embedded in your heart. The person is a part of you. Nothing can change that. You no longer need to give any thought or energy to trying to hold on to that person. That person and the love (or Essence of the person) is *always* with you. If thoughts about the situation or condition come to mind, know that you have already taken any blessings from the situation and that all the rest is gone.

Once you have released, it is important to claim to the Universe what you do want. You've released this person, situation or experience for a reason. You have lovingly released everything that doesn't serve you, and you now are free to claim the situation or experience that does serve you.

You may also want to affirm that you are worthy of receiving what you want and that you have proved your worth by lovingly releasing this person. You have shown a great act of self-love by standing firm in knowing what you deserve.

You may say, "I open myself up to experience a loving, supportive relationship, or I am now free to experience perfect health, energy and vitality." Or, "I am now open to receive the gifts of the Universe in the form of money, connections or resources."

Now give thanks in advance for what you have claimed for yourself. Act as if it has already happened. Know that at some level the process has already begun and the Universe has shifted to give you that which you desire. Know that what you have claimed for yourself is true for you and becomes your reality.

Congratulations! You have now released that which doesn't serve you, and you have opened up to new possibilities.

We have an audio version of this Releasing Meditation available at our Web site at: *www.lessonsfromarubberband.com.*

Chapter 20
The Path of Least Resistance

There is a concept in physics called the path of least resistance. It states that nature automatically flows where there is least resistance. We can apply the laws of nature to our own lives and learn to go with the flow.

Taking the path of least resistance doesn't necessarily mean that you won't encounter obstacles; it means that when you do, you will reevaluate the situation and gravitate toward the path of least resistance.

If things start to feel like a struggle or a fight, that indicates that you're *not* going with the flow. You've shut yourself off from the flow of life. You've taken your rubber band (your experiences) and twisted and contorted it until you've cut off the flow of life.

Eckhart Tolle states that "*all* suffering is due to resistance."

Think about some of the examples I used earlier. Let's say you're suffering at a dead-end job, day after day, trying to make ends meet. What are you resisting? Are you resisting the fact that this job may not be best suited for you? Or are you resisting another path that may be more compatible with your talent, skill, or passion?

Let's say you're constantly working on trying to *make* a relationship loving. What are you resisting? Are you resisting allowing yourself to experience peaceful relationships? Are you resisting the fact that this person may never change?

If you are struggling in any area of your life, take a look at what you are resisting. Then work on releasing.

Now, releasing doesn't necessarily mean you have to quit your job or break up with the person you're seeing. It just means giving up the suffering. It means going with the flow instead of against it. It means allowing life to work through you. The details will work themselves out naturally.

Sometimes people think I'm saying that if they are suffering or if things are hard work, to just let go and quit the job or quit the relationship; this isn't the truth. There's a difference between working at something and trying to *make* things happen, which we'll explore next.

Chapter 21
Hard Work or Resistance?

People often ask, "What is the difference between hard work and trying to *make* something happen?"

Most things take work, but it shouldn't feel like work or feel like you're trying to put a square peg into a round hole.

To illustrate this, I will give two examples, one from my relationship and one from work.

What is amazing about my current relationship with my husband is the willingness that we *both* have to work on it and to develop a loving, conscious relationship. We are both committed to the relationship, *and* we are both committed to our own personal growth. When things get rough or when we have differing views, we are able to really look at them from the perspective of working through them instead of giving up or moving on to another relationship.

Looking back at all my other relationships, I realize that I never had this *two*-sided type of love before. It was either me giving and putting in all the effort, or me not being interested.

But now, to have a relationship that is mutually caring, beneficial, loving, and committed is truly a treasure. I do not believe that *anyone* should settle for less than what he or she deserves. I know it is possible to have a wonderful, loving relationship that does flow and that doesn't feel like work.

I mentioned earlier that my past relationships were less than perfect, and yet I have learned and grown from each one. My past relationships always involved a lot of struggle, a lot of compromise, and a lot of giving up and sacrifice. I used to wonder why relationships were so much hard work. In my heart, I couldn't believe relationships should be such a struggle.

Yet people continually told me that relationships are hard work, and that it's supposed to be that way. I just couldn't believe that, yet I stayed in many relationships longer than I should have because I had bought into the theory that relationships are hard work.

One of my relationships before I met my husband was a constant struggle. I was always trying to make things work. But when I gave up trying to make things happen, the relationship naturally disintegrated, and we parted ways.

Now that I am in a wonderful, loving relationship, I realize that relationships do take work. Yes, they require maintenance, patience and compromise. But the difference is that it is doesn't *feel* like work. Let me compare it to this work analogy.

When I worked full-time in Nuclear Medicine, I worked my tail off. It was stressful, it was very technical, and a lot of things could go wrong on any given day. It was also labor intensive (e.g., getting patients to the imaging table). I worked really hard, and after years of doing this, I realized I didn't like my job. In fact, I began to loathe it. But again, I had bought into the theory that most people don't like their jobs and that's just the way it is.

When I quit my job in 2001 to pursue my writing career and my mission, I worked harder and longer hours than I ever worked in Nuclear Medicine.

I sometimes would go for weeks working twelve to fourteen hours a day or more. I would work at my computer all day, taking short breaks for lunch or dinner, and work into the wee hours of the morning.

It was more work than I ever did in Nuclear Medicine. A lot of it was even harder, in the sense that I often had to make cold calls to people to get speaking engagements, for example. I had to learn new skills in publishing, marketing, and more. All this was very hard work and took a lot more effort than I had ever put into my previous career.

The difference was that while it was hard work, it didn't *feel* like work. Yes, it took lots of time and effort, but I loved what I was doing.

Same with my relationship. Yes, it takes work. But we are both so committed to one another and so loving toward one another that it doesn't *feel* like work. It's just part of the upkeep in maintaining a strong relationship.

I don't believe life is meant to be a struggle. If it is a struggle, it is because we are making it that way. We are resisting something. But when we release, we flow with the river of life instead of trying to swim upstream in a fruitless attempt to make something work.

So if your relationship is hard work, ask yourself how you can release and allow the relationship to unfold. If your job is hard work, ask yourself how you can release and allow it to unfold.

But remember the distinction that everything takes work—relationships, careers, raising children—but that when it gets to the point that you feel as if you're trying to push a boulder up a hill, then it's time to try releasing and letting go. This may or may not mean quitting your job or leaving the relationship.

If you release and open yourself up to the flow of the Universe, the answer will become clear to you. The details will work themselves out. Life will unfold as it should.

Chapter 22
Decisions, Decisions

Most material written about success says that you have to be quick on your toes and know how to make immediate decisions.

I know that at times when I've needed to make an immediate decision, I was already leaning one way or another so I was able to make the decision with clarity and ease.

I also know that at times I have not been able to make a decision because I was oscillating back and forth between different scenarios. I was confused about which direction to take.

So what do I do with indecision? I just sit with it. Some success gurus may call this procrastination or indecisiveness; I call it wisdom.

It's about allowing the answer or direction to simply come to you. Albert Einstein once said, "When the solution is simple, God is answering."

I can't tell you how many times I was struggling with a decision and just decided to step back and wait for the answer to come to me, and it did!

Sometimes the answer comes in the form of a decision that is made for you (e.g., the job is already taken; the trip is already booked).

Most of the time, for me, it comes as complete clarity. Suddenly, I absolutely know what to do, it feels really perfect, and things absolutely flow.

If a decision is difficult and you're having a hard time figuring out what to do—don't *do* anything. This doesn't mean to be lazy and put off your decision or shove it under the rug. (Remember what happens when you do that?)

It just means to sit with the decision until the way becomes clear. Sometimes I affirm to myself, "I know the answer will appear to me at the right time and right place, and I know I will be divinely guided to take action one way or another."

When you allow the answer to unfold, you will soon know one way or another what to do. The answer will become apparent, and then you can make your decision with confidence.

Chapter 23

Listening to That Still, Small Voice

Last year my husband and I were planning for our wedding. Most importantly, we were also planning for our future together. I want to mention this because it seems that so many people plan for their wedding day more than they plan for their life together.

Anyway, Michael and I were talking about the issue of cold feet because we had just seen a news segment on television about a woman who was a runaway bride.

We couldn't really understand this phenomenon of cold feet. Neither of us was experiencing cold feet at the time nor had we ever had cold feet. Yet in movies or on television, this syndrome seems to be quite common. Many people say that it's normal to have cold feet.

I don't think it is normal to have cold feet. I think having cold feet indicates that something is wrong. It could either mean that you're unsure about *your partner*, or that you're just not ready to take the next step of a committed relationship *with anyone*.

If you have cold feet it's probably an indication that (1) you're not ready to get married at all or (2) you're not ready to get married to that particular person.

What is true for my husband and me is that neither of us had cold feet before our wedding. Yes, we were nervous about all the final arrangements and about how the ceremony would turn out, but we did not have any feelings of cold feet or doubts about spending our future together.

The point I'm trying to make *is to always trust your inner guidance.* If you feel something is not right, don't pretend that it is. Stop and listen to that still, small voice within.

If you have the feeling, "This isn't right, or something's not right," listen to it. If you have cold feet about anything, look at it instead of ignoring it.

What should you do if you have cold feet about something? Wait until you don't have cold feet. Postpone your decision until you can move forward without any reservations.

One of two things will happen. Your cold feet will go away and you'll be able to move forward with confidence; or your cold feet won't go away, and you'll have new realizations that may point you in a new direction that you're more confident about.

Always remember to listen to that still small voice within. If you have cold feet, or an uneasy feeling, it's an indication that something isn't right. Go within, listen to your inner wisdom, and wait patiently until you know exactly what to do.

Make a habit of checking in with yourself. Ask yourself: "What's going on inside my body?" Listen to that still, small voice.

Also be sure to pay attention to how your body feels. Does your body feel light and at ease or does it feel heavy and burdened? This will also give you an indication of how to proceed.

Listening to That Still, Small Voice

Some call that still, small voice within intuition. It doesn't matter what name you give it, but it is important to know that you have divine wisdom inside you. You have the answers.

Just check in with yourself and wait patiently until you know exactly what to do.

Chapter 24
Attached to Outcome

Sometimes we are so attached to a specific outcome that it seems as if the very things we are attached to become more and more elusive or are even repelled. That's because we have taken our situation (our rubber band) and cut off the flow of life with it.

If, instead, we could just release our attachment to a specific outcome, things would flow naturally and work out for our benefit anyway.

I have had two recent experiences in which I was *not* attached to the outcome and the greatest good unfolded naturally.

A while back, Mike Gerdes, a minister who has been very supportive of my work from the very beginning, gave me a call to tell me that he had nominated me for the 2006 Religious Science International Peace Award. But he also told me not to get my hopes up because the competition was very stiff.

I was honored to be nominated and didn't really think that I would win. I was not at all attached to the outcome. I figured that it would be great if I did get the award; and if I didn't, it would still be fine. I knew that I was having a positive impact on others and I didn't need an award to validate that.

However, a few years prior, there was a peace award at a church I was very involved with; everyone there knew how dedicated I was to peace, yet I did not win the award.

At that time, I had been attached to receiving the award. I felt as if I deserved it. I felt that I did more for peace than the person who received the award. I felt as if all my work wasn't being acknowledged or validated. I was coming from a place of pure ego, feeling that I needed outer validation for my work to be considered important. No wonder I didn't receive the award!

But this time, I felt blessed just to be nominated. In my heart I knew the importance of the work I was doing, and I didn't need any external validation.

So, guess what? I received the Peace Award and was presented with it in July 2006, at the Asilomar Conference in Monterrey, California. I am so thankful to have received it. It is icing on the cake so to speak. Yet my work isn't any more or less important than it was before I received the award.

I've had numerous situations in my life where when I was unattached to the outcome, it worked out for my highest benefit anyway.

Another experience happened recently regarding buying a house. As newlyweds, my husband and I were looking for our first home. I had spent months searching for houses in our price range. But unfortunately, because our budget was small, the houses we could afford were in dumpy neighborhoods or were falling apart.

We finally found one that had everything we were looking for in terms of size and features. At the

Attached to Outcome

time, the Portland, Oregon, real estate market was very competitive. Sellers were getting what they asked for, if not more. We submitted an offer meeting the seller's asking price. We also found out that there was another offer on the table.

We honestly didn't think we'd get the house. In fact, I told my husband that if we didn't, something else would turn up. We were both unattached to the outcome. We figured if we got it, we would be pleased, and if we didn't, we would find something better.

Well, guess what? We got the house. The owner accepted our offer.

But as it turned out, the house failed the inspection and we ended up not pursuing the deal. Yet we were completely unattached to the outcome and immediately went right back to looking for other houses. Shortly after, we found a beautiful home in a very nice neighborhood. We liked it better than the first home.

These two experiences remind me that when I just let go and allow things to unfold, they naturally work out for my highest and best good.

Practice being unattached to a specific outcome. I use these affirmations as a way of releasing my attachment to outcome: "I know that the situation is unfolding just as it should" or "I know that this situation is working out for my highest and greatest good."

Here are two other affirmations you might use: "I release and allow this situation to unfold as it should" or "I let go and allow the answer to express itself."

Most of us have heard the phrase "Let go, let God." When we let go, we clear the space for the Universe to work through us.

Chapter 25

Experiencing Joy

Instead of taking your rubber band and cutting off the flow of life, it's important to open up to the joy of life all around you.

Recently, I was interviewed by Barbara Rose of *Inspire Magazine* (*www.borntoinspire.com*). One of her interview questions was, "If you were to die tomorrow, what would you like to be known for?"

I started typing away (it was an E-mail interview) about how I would like to be known as a famous screenwriter who made really awesome movies or an author who really made a difference in the world or a speaker who pulled in huge audiences.

Then I stopped typing because I realized that what I *really* would want to be known for was the joy and love I brought into each situation.

I would want my husband to remember me for the joy we experienced together in every moment. I would want my colleagues to remember me for bringing joy into the situation. I would like my audience to remember me as someone who brought joy to my presentations.

I try to habitually ask myself, "Am I feeling joy in this moment?" If the answer is no, I then ask myself, "How can I bring joy into this moment?"

Again, when you ask how to do something, and you sit and wait for that inner wisdom to answer, you can trust that your answer is coming from Spirit.

Recently, I was in a situation in which I was not experiencing joy in the moment. I am co-owner of a business that helps to develop and market products for real estate investing, and one day I realized that I wasn't really experiencing joy in our meetings. Primarily, it was because of one person I didn't really get along with (which I'll talk about in part three).

Anyway, I started to dread going to the meetings. Once I realized I was not experiencing joy in our meetings, I asked myself, "How can I bring joy into this situation?"

The answer that came to me was that I should simply be my normal, cheerful, playful self. I had been showing up at these meetings with a "let's get things done" attitude and I really had been hard-nosed.

Yet, at home and around friends, I'm constantly singing and being silly. So I decided to change the way I behaved at the meetings.

While driving to the next meeting, I listened to some great music. And as always, I got a song stuck in my head. But instead of suppressing it and acting professional, I walked in singing it. *"I'm too sexy for my cat, too sexy for my cat, so sexy it hurts,"* I sang.

Before I knew it, one of the other guys was singing the song too, and the meeting turned out to be very productive and fun.

Now, I'm not saying you have to go into a meeting singing a silly song. That may or may not work for you. But for me, that's part of who I am. So it was natural to go in singing and being silly.

Experiencing Joy

After the meeting, we attend a class where I record the materials of the experts. One of the women in the class said, "You seem different tonight. You seem really happy."

So now I make a habit of asking, "Am I experiencing joy in this moment?" And if not, "How can I bring joy into this moment?"

I encourage you to ask yourself this question daily. And if you are not experiencing joy in a situation, ask yourself what you can do to bring more joy into the moment.

At my speaking engagements, this is where I normally get questions from the audience about what to do if they can't bring joy into that moment.

If you can't find ways to bring joy into your current situation, then maybe you need to re-evaluate your current situation.

For example, toward the later part of my career in medicine, I was not experiencing joy. I would ask myself, "How can I bring joy into this moment?" I came up with all kinds of answers that I could act on: by incorporating writing time into my schedule, by allowing more quiet time for myself, by getting a massage, by moving to another hospital where they had a bigger department and more support staff.

But what I ultimately realized was that no matter what I did, I could not bring joy to that moment, that experience of my career. After a while I realized I could bring joy into my life by not working in that field full time anymore.

I'm not saying people should go out and quit their jobs; what I am saying is that if you can't find a way to experience joy in your current situation (whether it be a relationship, a job, or something else), then you may need to find a way to experience joy in *another* situation.

I decided to pursue my passion for writing only after six years of *not* experiencing joy in my current career. Now I experience joy every day, being able to do what I love. I will discuss my career change in more detail in part three.

Again, it's important to start paying attention to your feelings, to get in touch with your true self, and then act from that place of wisdom.

Bring the joy of your being into every moment.

Chapter 26

Passive Peace

Until now, I've been talking about learning to go with the flow of life—to release and let go, and try not to *make* things happen. I've been talking about *not* twisting your rubber band and cutting off the flow of life.

But it could be said that great leaders like Gandhi and Martin Luther King worked hard to *make* things happen in regard to social injustice.

Yes, these leaders did *make* positive changes in the world but they did so from the level of being. They made profound changes from that level. They combined their being with action. Action without being is futile. Change occurs at the level of being more than doing.

For my first book, *Peaceful Earth: Spiritual Perspectives on Inner Peace and World Peace,* I compiled a Top 10 list of things that we can *do* to create peaceful lives, peaceful relationships, and a peaceful earth. Although there are little things we can do daily, the lasting results come from the little doings that help us get to that place of *being* peace.

That's why Gandhi said "Be the change you wish to see" instead of "*Do* the change you wish to see."

Often, people who hear these comments get the impression that I'm recommending not doing anything.

While I believe that peace will come from a shift in consciousness, I also believe that there are certain things that can be done at the level of form to create a more peaceful climate.

But the distinction is to *do* these things from a place of *being*.

Again, if I try to *make* something happen, I am in the energy of opposing or fighting something. Ironically, that is often the same energy I am trying to dispel.

To solve any problem, shine the light of your Essence (Consciousness) into the situation. Yes, action may then be inspired out of this place of consciousness, but you work from this level of being.

For example, I am appalled at the crisis in Darfur. When I hear about the genocide I get angry and I complain. But when I go within, I come up with appropriate solutions to help in my own way, like donating 10% of the profits of this book to organizations that help ease the crisis in Darfur, as well as other organizations. (Read more in the Epilogue). When I come from this place of being, I am much more effective in the world.

We can look at the issue of cause and effect to understand this concept more deeply. Eckhart Tolle, in the *Power of Now*, says all evil is the result of unconsciousness and that war is the result of mass unconsciousness. War and violence are the *effects*. The *cause* is unconsciousness.

("Unconsciousness" here refers to feeling separate from our Source and acting from the ego, mind, pain-body or Imposter).

To produce change, people must work at the level of cause and effect simultaneously. (Though change can happen solely from the level of cause; which we'll see in a moment.)

So the cause of war, hatred, violence, and so forth is unconsciousness. How do we solve this problem? By shining the light of our consciousness into the situation.

Again, we cannot create change by fighting against something or by carrying that energy of fighting something. If we carry that energy of fighting or resistance, we are actually feeding the very thing we are trying to solve. We are polarizing the opposite energy, and making it bigger.

This is what Einstein meant when he said you can't solve a problem from the same level of thinking that created the problem. The problem is unconsciousness, and we can't solve the problem by being unconscious. The solution will come from a level of consciousness.

Now, again, some people don't particularly want to hear this because they believe they must *do* something to save the world. And yes, this is very noble. But the change will come from your consciousness, or being, *uniting* with your doing.

Let's take Mother Teresa as the ultimate example of how one person acting from the place of being affects positive change. Her influence on healing the lives of others was the result of her *being*, not her *doing*. Yes, she did form missionaries all over the world and train people to heal and help the broken-hearted, the sick, and the destitute. She influenced many decision makers and raised lots of money.

But Mother Teresa herself claimed that there was often nothing she could *do* for people, but that her greatest gift was just to *be* with people. She didn't concern herself with things of the world because her contribution occurred at the level of being.

And while Mother Teresa became very politically active in her final years, her greatest accomplishments were from the acts of being that she demonstrated with the people she helped every day. This is what Mother Teresa is known and remembered for. She is known for her simple acts of giving love to those who needed it. This love came from her Essence, from her being.

Eckhart Tolle says, "You teach through being, through demonstrating the peace of God. You become the 'light of the world,' an emanation of pure consciousness, and so you eliminate suffering on the level of cause. You eliminate unconsciousness from the world."

Darkness cannot exist in the presence of light. Hate cannot exist in the presence of love. War cannot exist in the presence of peace.

And this all starts in your own consciousness. Shine your light, your love, and your peace into the world. You can still *do* things on a daily basis to create positive change, but do some from a place of being.

Chapter 27
Imposing Your Will on Someone Else

Not only do we try to *make* things happen in our own lives, but we also often try to *make* others conform to our will. And when we do this to others, it cuts off our life flow just as when we do it to ourselves. It is equivalent to taking the rubber band and twisting it around our wrist.

Just as it is necessary to release trying to *make* things happen for ourselves, it is also important to release trying to make someone else conform to our intentions or wishes.

We often, with good intentions, try to *make* others do what we think they should do or what we think is in their best interests.

My husband is a very talented drummer. Before we met, he was in a band that performed some local shows and even produced a CD.

In my opinion, my husband was the best player in the band. I didn't think the vocalist was very good, and I thought the other players were mediocre. My husband's mom agreed.

It's always been my philosophy to get with the best and to push myself to be even better. I shared my philosophy with my husband, and eventually, through his own realizations, he left that band and started working on demos to audition for a more talented working band. But I didn't force him to do this. He had to make the decision on his own. I just kept expressing my belief in him.

Unfortunately, he didn't leave the band on good terms. He had basically been the bank for the band, to fund the CD. The other members were going to pay him back, but since he left the band, they ended up not making payments. They no longer felt obligated to pay him back.

And on top of that, they had all the CDs. Plus, they blamed me for being the reason he left, so they weren't on great speaking terms.

This really angered me, because I felt that my husband had been taken advantage of. I thought that if he could at least recoup the CDs, we could sell them on E-bay and at least make some of the money back.

I kept encouraging him to contact the other band members. I even told him we could show up at their house and take back the CDs. And I brought up the idea of small claims court. I thought he had been taken advantage of, and I wanted him to not stand for it.

But one day, my husband said to me, "I just want to let it go. What's done is done. I just want to move on."

But I wanted him to move on *after* we recouped some of his money. I wanted him to not let those guys get away with what they did. And yet, my husband just wanted to let things go.

I realized that I was imposing my will—my anger—on him. Ultimately, I want my husband to be at

Passive Peace

peace with the situation. He said he would be at peace by just letting it go and moving on. But I wasn't.

I had to learn to release *my need* for him to get his money back from these guys. I needed to let my husband deal with the situation in his own way.

It's true my husband asks me for advice on things, as I ask him. But giving advice is different from trying to *make* someone do something you think they should do.

We are only responsible for our own responses. I had to release the situation and allow him to handle it in his own way. I love him and somehow thought that by forcing him to do something, I was looking out for his best interests. But in reality, it became about me, not about him.

My best advice to him would have been to do what he needed to do to be at peace with the situation.

My husband released the situation and hasn't thought about it since. But when we have to pay an unexpected bill, I still have the thought that he should try to get his CDs back so we can recoup some of our money. I still have to practice releasing.

I learned in a powerful way that you can't *make* others do something that you want them to do. Everyone has to find his or her own way.

So instead of imposing my will on him, I release him, knowing that he is capable of making decisions for himself. I affirm that he has divine wisdom within him, and knows for himself what is best for him.

PART THREE:

How to Stop Hurting Yourself with Your Rubber Band

Chapter 28
Living from the Inside Out

We live in a material world. Today, thousands of companies claim we will be happy if we buy their products. When you turn on the television you hear that if you buy this certain makeup, you will be beautiful and that of course will make you happy. Or if you use this particular program to lose weight, you will be happy. Or if you purchase this money-making program, you will be happy because you will be able to buy so much more stuff. Or if you use these techniques, you will be able to attract your soul mate, and then you will be happy.

We've all heard and seen these infomercials and commercials, right? And I'm just as much a sucker as anyone else. I've been sucked into the programs, convinced that if I just got that new makeup, I'd be happy. Or I'd go on a shopping splurge convinced that if I had that new wardrobe, I'd be happy.

I had done this for years with my relationships. If I had this certain relationship I'd be happy. Then when I was in that relationship, I wasn't happy. But that was okay because if I had this other type of relationship, I'd be happy. And on and on and on . . . I even moved to a different physical location thinking if I moved to this city, I'd be happy.

How many of us spend most of our lives thinking about things that would make us happy? If only I had "this," then I'd be happy!

From the previous examples, we can see that happiness is often based on externals (this or that product or house or car or romance). It is the belief that we need something physical or a certain thing to make us happy. This is a false belief because really many of the very things we thought would make us happy no longer make us happy at some point.

That new outfit that you bought just three weeks ago that made you so happy is now out of style and doesn't make you happy. Or the happiness that resulted from that new house suddenly wears off when you see your first mortgage bill.

The difference between "happiness" and "inner peace" is that one is externally driven and one is internal.

Happiness is primarily sought after through external means—whereas inner peace comes from that inner place of being.

When we seek happiness we are seeking something outside ourselves to make us happy. I think that part of the key to inner peace is to live from the inside out—living from that place of remembering our connection with our Source.

The idea is to get to the place of being internally aware and focused instead of being externally driven and motivated (for things).

Any time we fall victim to outer circumstances, we are metaphorically snapping ourselves with our rubber bands. We continue to hurt ourselves if we base our life on externals.

Living From the Inside Out

At the level of externals, things constantly change. Someone is born, someone dies. Someone enters your life, someone leaves. Money comes and goes. Things come and go.

You cannot be happy when the boyfriend leaves, the money goes away, or the friend betrays you, although you *can* experience inner peace.

There is a center of peace inside of you that remains no matter what is going on externally. And you can always tap into it.

I had always wanted *the* relationship and thought that I would be really happy when I had it. But what I eventually learned was that I had to experience inner peace without the relationship before I could attract it, and that is exactly what happened.

Previously, I talked about meeting my life partner after releasing a situation that didn't serve me. When I released what didn't serve me, I felt a great love for myself and experienced intense joy and inner peace on my own, which I write about in the following chapters.

But how do we tap into that place of peace? On the next page is a poem I wrote about living from the inside out. The next few chapters will show us how to live from the inside out. They will show us how to stop snapping ourselves with our rubber bands and experience inner peace no matter what is going on externally.

Living from the Inside Out

Living from the Inside Out,
I know this is what life is truly about.

Seems I'm always searching for happiness
outside myself,
like that new car, new outfit, or other
external wealth.

Searching for the right person to fill me up
inside,
running from one location to another,
trying to find a place to hide.

Looking for a place to hide from my pain,
an instant cure-all, an external band aid, a
point to gain.

I am helpless, often feeling out of control,
paying attention to people, places, and things
instead of listening to my soul.

Waiting for that perfect moment to come,
instead of enjoying the one I have and
basking in the sun.

Trying to make something happen by force
instead of trusting in the fact that I am right
on course.

Living From the Inside Out

If I just remember that I'm right where I
need to be
and know that Divine Intelligence is
shining through me,

If I can live my life each day
excited about the miraculous part I'm here
to play,

Remembering that all the wisdom I need
to see
is always right inside of me,

Remembering that all I desire, want,
and need
has already been planted in me like a seed,

A seed that needs the nourishment of
knowing,
that this God seed inside me is always
growing

The love, peace, happiness, and health I
wish to see
is really the ultimate Truth of me.

My purpose in life is to learn to live from
the inside,
where the perfect expression of God
resides.

Chapter 29

Reactive or Responsive?

Do you ever feel like a ball in a pinball game? Bouncing back and forth, reacting to one stimulus after another? Most of us, including myself at times, are so busy reacting to external stimuli instead of responding from our inner guidance.

Does this sound like you?

Someone says something to you that could be construed as negative, and you react to them by saying something damaging or hurtful? Or, you see the next new fad (outfit, offer or gimmick), and you know you just *have to have it* because it will solve all your problems?

I can be as reactionary as anyone; that's why I believe part of my practice is to *teach* peace, and at the same time, learn these lessons for myself. Yet, I also know that when I live from the inside out, I am less reactionary to circumstances in my life.

Recently, I received an E-mail from a business partner that I perceived as derogatory towards me. Of course, I started firing back. I just let go. I let everything pour out of me about how it was this person's fault for everything. I really let him have it! I felt totally justified, and I quickly hit the "send" button. Have you ever done that and immediately wished you could delete the E-mail, but it was too late?

Well, that's what happened to me. I regretted sending the E-mail, but once I hit "send" there was nothing I could do. And, of course, it led to a whole series of miscommunications. Had I waited and responded from a place of centeredness, I'm sure the outcome would have been different.

That's the difference between reacting and responding. Reacting is where we just act immediately to defend ourselves or attack someone else. It's like the "fight or flight" response. It's full of emotion. It's behaving from our emotions.

Responding is going within, and listening to that, still, small voice, and coming up with our solution from a place of centeredness. Responding is taking our emotion out of the scenario. Responding is contemplative thought without emotion.

Another way to say this is; a reaction is externally driven whereas a response is internally focused.

Being reactive is being a *victim* to your circumstances. It's like being that pinball tossed around from one place to another.

Do you want to continue to be a victim to your circumstances or do you want to be able to respond to situations from a place of wisdom and centeredness? And, how do we learn to respond instead of react?

I will offer two simple solutions that have really worked for me. Other solutions such a breathing, meditation and prayer will be discussed in the following chapters.

Creating a Response Policy

Ever notice how Department stores have Return Policies and Web sites have Privacy Policies? Well, what if individuals or groups had Response Policies?

I decided to create a Response Policy for myself in advance so I would be able to appropriately handle situations where I tend to be reactive.

Here is my Response Policy:
I will wait 24 hours before acting on something, whether it be an E-mail or an offer.

I basically allow 24 hours to pass before I do anything. For example, in the case of the derogatory E-mail I received, I still may write that reactive E-mail and tell the person what I really feel, but then I save it as a draft and let 24 hours pass. Then I look at it 24 hours later and if I choose to send it I will at that time. But most of the time, I'm thankful that I didn't send the E-mail.

For me, it can be therapeutic to go ahead and vent my frustrations in an E-mail or letter, but not to send it since it is based on my reaction and not my response.

I also have created this same policy with my buying patterns. In the past, I have been so reactive to any offer that involves bettering my career or business.

Often I'd get an E-mail on "how to build your speaking career" and I just felt like I had to buy it. I'd convince myself that if I bought just this one course, I'd be successful.

I can't tell you how many programs I have sitting on my shelf regarding creating a successful business. And yes, some of them have been very beneficial, but most of them haven't been the answer that I thought they would be when I bought them.

For example, if I see something that I know I just "have to have", I tell myself that I choose to wait 24 hours; and if I still feel like I would like this particular item after the waiting period, then, at that time, I will give myself permission to buy it. Many times, after 24 hours, I don't even want the item anymore.

Now, I understand that many things can't wait 24 hours. What if you are feuding with a spouse, co-worker or family member? It's unrealistic to think that you could wait 24 hours before doing anything in this type of situation. That's where you create an Immediate Response Policy.

For example, early on in our relationship my husband and I worked out an agreement in advance that if we got angry with one another we would call a "time out" and physically separate ourselves by having him go upstairs and me stay downstairs for at least 15 minutes to allow ourselves to blow off steam and center ourselves. Ironically since we've implemented the plan we've never had to use it. But it is there in case we need it.

I invite you to make a Response Policy for yourself that helps you respond instead of react. For example, if you're in a difficult situation where there are a lot of emotions, give yourself the space to be able to respond. Maybe make a policy like mine where you wait 24 hours before you respond to an E-mail.

Also, you may want to make a policy to not buy things on impulse. Make an agreement with yourself that if you still feel you desire the item after 24 hours, then you are free to buy it. You'd be amazed at all the stuff we feel we just absolutely need, and 24 hours later we're wondering why we even wanted the item in the first place. This experiment is very revealing on how much stuff we buy with our emotions!

Next, create an Immediate Response Policy at work or with your family members that maps out in advance what you will do in a time of crisis. For example, if an argument arises and the situation gets uncomfortable, call a "time out" and move away from the situation for a specified amount of time.

Directing your Awareness to your Center

Often, the difference between reacting and responding means moving out of our heads (our minds or egos) and going within (connecting with our center).

The Solar Plexus area (located about two fingers above your navel) is a place of personal power. It is the place of intuition. It is your core, your center. It is a place of knowing.

I have found it very beneficial to place my hand over my Solar Plexus area to remind me to bring my awareness out of my head (mind) and into my core.

By doing this simple gesture, I have learned to go within and check with my inner self, instead of reacting to my emotions.

In my speaking career, I've noticed a huge difference between reacting and responding when I focus my awareness on my Solar Plexus area.

Public speaking has been one of my greatest fears. Even now, I always have some nervous energy right before my talks. Fortunately I can channel it into excitement but it is still reactive energy. It's still the "fight or flight" response. In this emotional state, the pace of my speech is fast and I pace from side to side; it's like watching a tennis match. And it "works" for various parts of my speeches.

But there are other times when I focus on speaking from my belly (my Solar Plexus area) and I find I am more centered and can communicate more effectively. This is my *powerhouse*. When I speak from my Solar Plexus area, I am grounded. Often, I'll put my hand over my belly to remind me to speak from my center.

I notice also, that putting my hand on my belly reminds me to speak from my center in one-on-one conversations as well. If I feel like I'm getting agitated with a person, I can put my hand on my belly, take a deep breath and respond from my center.

Try this experiment now. Talk out loud about something exciting. Either stand in front of a mirror or talk to a friend. (Of course tell them what you are doing and ask them to note your tone and behavior).

Reactive or Responsive?

Get really involved in the emotions you're feeling, and talk about the situation, item or experience in detail.

Now put your hand on your belly and talk about that same situation, but speak through your belly. Notice a difference? Ask your partner or friend if he/she notices a difference between the two scenarios.

I've done this on the phone before. I'll start talking to a friend I haven't talked to in a while. And when I'm really excited and reactive (full of emotions) my voice is really high pitched.

Then I'll notice how anxious I am and I'll put my hand on my belly and continue talking to them from this place. The difference is astounding. Most often, people tell me I communicate better when I'm speaking from my core.

Sometimes just putting your hand over your belly reminds you to breathe deeply through your belly and could mean the difference between reacting and responding. I will discuss breathing through your belly in the following chapters.

Next time you feel reactive, try to bring your awareness into your Solar Plexus area, and notice how your energy changes.

Once you become more responsive and less reactive, you'll notice a tremendous improvement in your life and your relationships.

Chapter 30
Take a Deep Breath!

Let's face it: most of us are in reaction mode. We're constantly reacting to our environment, we're stressed out, we're busy, we're overwhelmed, we're operating from a level of fear, and yet if we took time to just *breathe*, things could be much better—we could respond from a place of centeredness. We could stop snapping ourselves with our rubber bands.

Eastern religions, martial arts, and yoga have long realized the power of deep breathing. Taking full deep breaths increases our circulation and mental clarity. It also gives us more *time* to compose ourselves and to step out of the problem instead of initially reacting.

Deep breathing helps us live from the internal rather than the external. Living from this space means that whatever happens externally, we are okay. Gandhi said that "peace to be real, must be unaffected by outside circumstances." Breathing and meditation help us to *not* be affected by our outer circumstances and to come from that innermost place of peace.

Yet most of us aren't even breathing adequately or taking the time to get the full benefits of deep breathing. Take a deep breath right now.

Where did you feel it? If you felt it in your chest, you are doing what is called shallow breathing. You're not supplying your brain or internal organs with the optimum amount of oxygen. You're not receiving the full benefits of a breath.

When I first tried this exercise, I realized that most of my life I had been shallow breathing from my chest. Eastern traditions stress the importance of breathing through your belly. This type of breathing has been called belly breathing or even Buddha breathing.

Here is a technique to breathe from your belly and to receive the benefits of a full breath.

Technique for Breathing through your Belly

Place one or both hands on the area around your navel. Now imagine your belly as a balloon. As you inhale, feel your belly rise like a balloon inflating, and as you exhale feel your belly lower as if the balloon is deflating. Do this a few times. Remember: as you inhale, you should feel your belly rise; and as you exhale, you should feel your belly lower.

I encourage you to practice this type of breathing every day, especially during times of stress. You can do this breathing exercise anywhere—in your car in traffic, before a meeting, or before responding to a question.

As you continue to practice deep breathing, you will find yourself with more energy, thinking more clearly, and able to respond to your life situations from a place of inner calmness.

Chapter 31
Meditation

Another powerful technique for living from the inside out, and being less reactive and more responsive is meditation.

Many meditation techniques incorporate deep breathing by focusing on following your breath as you inhale and exhale or just sitting silently and concentrating on your breath. For most meditations, breath work is very important.

There are many meditation books, CDs and guided meditations on the market. I encourage you to spend some time learning different techniques to find out which works best for you. (I have created a series of three guided meditations for experiencing inner peace, peaceful relationships, and world peace. You can find them at *www.lessonsfromarubberband.com*)

I will share a couple of meditations that have been very powerful for me.

One meditation I like, which has been mentioned by many great masters, is to go inside your body—to tap into that internal, eternal energy. This meditation takes you out of your mind (the root of all problems) and into your body.

On the next page is a summary of the technique.

Meditation for Going Inside Your Body

Start this meditation after you have done some deep breathing and when you're in a relaxed, comfortable position. Focus your attention and awareness on your feet. Try to feel the energy of your feet. After you have focused your attention on your feet, you can journey upward through your body by focusing next on your calves, your thighs, your abdomen, and so forth.

What does it mean to focus your attention on your feet or feel the energy of your feet? This gave me difficulty at first.

A good question to ask yourself if you're finding it difficult to bring your awareness to your feet (mentioned by Eckhart Tolle in *Gateway to the Now*) is, "Without moving or touching my right foot, how do I know my right foot exists?" Ask yourself that question and see if you can just feel the energy of your right foot. This question brings you into the awareness of your foot; it allows you to feel the energy of your foot.

Another good question taught by Buddhist monks is, "What's going on inside my body?" and to just feel what's going on in your inner body.

As you continue to do this meditation, you will become more centered and less reactive. Going inside your body and feeling its energy is a very powerful meditation. A few times that I've done it, I've actually felt as if I was invisible, as if I was pure energy. I had a sense of eternalness.

Meditation

Connecting through the Breath

Earlier I mentioned that the key to inner peace is remembering our connection with our Source. A way to do this is to connect through the breath. It goes like this:

As you inhale, say, "God is . . ."
As you exhale, say, "I am . . ."

Replace the " . . ." with a quality that you believe describes God. (I use "God" in this example, but in part four I will discuss honoring all beliefs and how we should not be attached to a "name.")

For example, as you inhale, you might say, "God is infinite," and as you exhale, you might say, "I am infinite."

Some of you may question the relatedness of God and yourself. But I like to think of it as a metaphor I've heard: If God is the ocean, you are the wave. Ultimately we are expressions of God. All the qualities of God are contained within us. God is infinite, I am infinite.

Again, it's important to find a way to tap into that "God energy" whether it's connecting through the breath, deep breathing, meditation, or guided meditation. Find what works for you and do it daily.

Chapter 32

Affirmative Prayer

The two most powerful techniques to use to live from the inside out are meditation (including breathing) and prayer. When we live from the inside out, we are less reactive, meaning we don't take our rubber bands and snap ourselves with them.

Later in part three, I will explore more ways to help you stop hurting yourself with your rubber band, ways such as accepting yourself and expressing yourself.

A powerful way to connect with our Source is through prayer. Now again, when I use the word "connect" I am using it in terms of "remembering our connection," because we are *always* connected with our Source (God); sometimes we just *forget*.

I have found affirmative prayer to be a way for me to remember my connection with God.

Another way of looking at affirmative prayer is this:

> "Just for a moment imagine that you are experiencing an unpleasant night dream: You are in the ocean, swimming; you have gone out too far; you look back toward the shore and see that there is very little hope of rescue. Even though you shout your lungs out, no one can hear you. And so you are seized with fear. You struggle and strive to reach the shore, and, of course, the harder you fight, the harder the ocean fights you. There is only one thing left for you to do—drown. Yes, drown—but wait!

In your fight, you shouted and someone heard you, came over and shook you, woke you up, and behold the miracle! The drowning self disappeared; the ocean disappeared; the struggle disappeared. You awakened and found that you had never left your comfortable home. All that was necessary in order to be released from the struggle was to AWAKEN."

—Joel Goldsmith
The Art of Spiritual Healing

Affirmative Prayer, simply, is an affirmation of the Truth beyond our human circumstances or experiences.

It can be stated so clearly as in Joel Goldsmith's explanation previously. We may be experiencing something at the human level of form, but all we need to do is to wake up to the truth beyond the form—the truth of that infinite potential that resides within each and every one of us.

The key to affirmative prayer is to recognize, affirm, and experience your Essence beyond your human experience. Truly, from this standpoint, nothing needs to be healed, only revealed.

In the Bible it says, "If you knew who walked beside you, you would never fear again." When we live and have our being in the consciousness of God, all is well. It is only when we forget who we are that problems arise.

Many people have grown up believing that prayer was a way of petitioning God, a way of trying

Affirmative Prayer

to get something that you really wanted. That's why many of us who have subscribed to that type of prayer have wound up asking, "Why doesn't God answer my prayers?" That very question in and of itself implies that our prayers are not answered. Petitioning prayer places the power outside us. In the Bible it says, "The Kingdom of Heaven is within." This is the place of all that is infinite.

We have learned from quantum physics that the world is but a reflection of what we see. If we see abundance, we experience abundance. If we see health, we experience health. The Universe actually bends, shapes, and shifts to reflect back to us what we see. (More on this in part four.)

The purpose of affirmative prayer is to see with "God vision," and not our limited human vision.

The other problem with the supplication or petitioning prayer is that by praying *for* something we are admitting to our lack of the very thing we are praying for.

In the Bible it says that if you pray and "act as if," all things will be provided. Joel Goldsmith says that "the only effective prayer is the attainment of God Realization."

The key here is to acknowledge that everything required for your abundance, health, success, love, and joy is already operating within you.

This is where most people have difficulty. During sorrow or pain or rough times, it can be hard to see with "God vision." Sometimes we can get so wrapped up in our own drama that we cannot see anything beyond it. It is difficult for us to know that what we are experiencing is not the truth of ourselves.

I had an experience a while back in which a girlfriend of mine was visiting and watching television while I had to finish something on the computer. The television was tuned to the Discovery channel. I peaked over and saw dolphins. Then I heard some dramatic music and saw the dolphins swimming fast. I just knew that a shark or a whale was about to attack.

I turned back to my computer because I don't like seeing dolphins, or any other animal, being hurt. Yet I could still hear the sounds in the background. I heard the dolphins squeal in pain. I heard thrashing in the water. I was having images of blood filling the water, like in those *Jaws* movies. I finally couldn't take it anymore and left the room in anger.

My girlfriend noticed and asked me what was wrong. I said, "I can't stand to watch animals being attacked by other animals. I couldn't bear watching it or even hearing it."

Then she said, "What do you mean? The show was about the dolphins' mating patterns."

This was a clear example of how our minds can play havoc with us. I had this whole traumatic event worked out in my head, and believed it to be the truth, when in reality the show was about one of the most loving acts in the world.

Sometimes, when we are in the middle of our pain, it may be difficult to see the truth. This is why spiritual practitioners, ministers, or consciousness

Affirmative Prayer

coaches are very effective. They can affirm the truth for you when you can't see it.

But ideally, you can learn to elevate your vision so that no matter what is going on externally, you know and affirm the truth internally.

Scientific prayer, or affirmative prayer, is an effective tool in revealing the truth beyond our experiences. "Prayer is a rising in consciousness above that which can be seen, heard, touched or smelled in order to perceive that which is real," says Joel Goldsmith.

Scientific or affirmative prayer, as I learned it, contains five steps. We will explore each step below. As with meditation, it is important to find something that works for you. The five steps aren't absolutely necessary but have been found to work for many people. Again, use this tool only if it works for you.

I've heard it said that prayer doesn't change God, it changes you. Find a tool that works for you to help you develop your "God vision" over your limited human vision.

Here are the five steps of affirmative prayer.

One: Recognition—God is.

This step is a recognition of what God is. (Again, I am using the term "God" but you can substitute any term from your particular religious belief instead.)

Often during this step, any synonym that describes the nature of God is used. God is the Infinite

Energy of the Universe. God is the One Presence, and One Power in the Universe. God is Eternal Life, God is abundance, God is perfection, God is wholeness, God is Life, Consciousness, Being. God is Harmony. God is the Creative Principle.

Two: Unification—I am.

This step is the affirmation that you are *one* with God. The Kingdom of Heaven is within. All that God is—you are. So for example, I am a divine expression of God.

I am abundant, I am infinite, I am perfect, I am peace, I am wisdom, I am clarity, I am eternal, I am creative.

Three: Realization or Affirmation—
The truth is.

This is the step in which you acknowledge the truth of the situation. In this step you can acknowledge the problem, but then acknowledge the truth. Sometimes this is important when saying a prayer for yourself when you are in the middle of a personal drama. You may at this point say, "I know that no matter what is happening in my life, the Law of God is operating within me right now."

In this step, you place the affirmation for your prayer. It is best to state the affirmations in the positive, present tense. It is important to stay away from affirmations such as "I know the truth that abundance will come to me." According to the law of the Universe, abundance is already available at every

Affirmative Prayer

moment. It is not "coming" to you but "expressing" as you.

Here is a powerful example of what might be included in this step, taken from Joel Goldsmith's book *The Art of Spiritual Healing*:

> These states of limitation do not exist. They are merely images of the mind—appearances—but the Truth is that the kingdom of God, the realm of eternal life and harmony is within me. It is not to be achieved; it is already within me. Because of this, I can always turn within and come into the full realization of the Kingdom, now. My only function is to become aware of its is-ness, to realize that it already is, and therefore I have nothing to seek.

Many people spend a lot of time in the third step because it is very important to fully affirm the ultimate truth.

I know the truth that God is my Source. The Infinite Law is always working through me, as me. I know that regardless of my situation or experience at the moment, there is a presence, a power working here, whether I see it or not. I know that the Universe is abundant and that I am an abundant being. I know that I do not need to give thought to financial concerns, because all that I need is already provided. I know that the infinite well resides within me and is working right now to bring about the highest good.

Four: Thanksgiving—I give thanks . . .

Giving thanks is a way of acknowledging the good in your life. Keeping with the prayer on abundance above, here's an example of this step:

I give thanks in advance for all the resources, contacts, connections that are available to fulfill my highest destiny. I give thanks for knowing that I am always supported, and the universal law is constantly working within me.

Five: Release—Let Go.

This is an important step because once you have said your prayer, by affirming the God qualities, realizing that you are one with those God qualities, claiming the truth, and giving thanks, it is time to release the prayer because it is already so.

During this step it can be tempting to go back to the original prayer request, which may be one to correct a feeling of lack. Sometimes people will say, "I release this prayer knowing that I am not lacking anything." This is the equivalent of planting a seed and then digging it up to see if it is growing. Once you have planted the seed, it is done. You can release it.

Prayer after all is just a realization of the truth, so you don't need to go back to the illusion.

An effective way to release is just to end by saying, "I release this prayer, knowing that it is already done."

These five steps are tools to help us stay in the consciousness of God. The order in which you use them or even whether you use all of them does not matter. These are just *tools* to train ourselves to stay in that higher consciousness, that place where all our relationships, finances, and health are perfect, whole, and complete in every way.

Chapter 33
Affirmation Basics

Affirmations are powerful tools to help us recognize and remember the truth. Again, they are not to be used as denials of our experience but as a realization of the ultimate Truth beyond our human experiences.

Here are some important points about using and creating affirmations.

*Use the present tense:
Instead of "I will be abundant," affirm "I am abundant."

*State affirmations in the positive:
Instead of saying "I am *not* sick," use the positive "I am healthy."

*Affirm what you desire instead of what you do not wish to experience. This is similar to the previous point. Instead of saying "I avoid negative people," state "I attract positive, healthy relationships into my life."

*Avoid the words "want" or "hope." These words imply "lack." Instead of saying "I want a relationship," say "I allow myself to experience a relationship." Instead of saying "I hope I get the job," affirm "I know that I will get the job if it is in my highest and greatest interest."

*See the affirmation as already fulfilled. Mere rote memorization of affirmations is not as effective as those that contain the belief, feelings, and sensations of an already fulfilled desire. Remember the adage "Act as if . . ." or the Bible verse that says whatever you ask for, believe that you have received it and it will be given to you.

*Basically, replace whatever you are seeing or experiencing with a God quality or the ultimate Truth. For example, I may be seeing or experiencing a lack of money. Yet, I also know that the Universe is abundant. This would be my affirmation: "The Universe is abundant."

If for some reason you can't see the God quality or the ultimate truth, as in the case of an illness or a tragedy, just affirm "I know that a greater truth exists in this situation," or "I am open and receptive to discovering the highest good in this situation."

*Anytime a negative thought or a belief in limitation occurs, immediately respond with your affirmation. Cancel the negative belief, and replace it with your affirmation.

Affirmation Basics

*Incorporate affirmations into your prayer and meditation. Repeat affirmations consistently throughout the day.

Again, it is important to make sure *not* to use affirmations as a form of denial. It is important to honor your feelings at the moment, and then elevate your vision beyond your feelings to the ultimate Truth. Affirmations can help in this process.

Chapter 34

Loving Yourself

Part of the process of experiencing inner peace every day comes from loving ourselves *and* expressing ourselves.

When we treat ourselves with love, kindness, and gentleness, we are honoring who we really are and thereby we experience inner peace. When we fully express ourselves and all that we are meant to be, we experience peace.

When we treat ourselves unfairly, unkindly, or disrespectfully we are snapping ourselves with our rubber bands. When we do not honor our true expression, we are snapping ourselves with our rubber bands. Ultimately, we are hurting ourselves.

First, I'm going to explain the process of loving ourselves; after that, I'll go into detail about expressing ourselves.

Loving ourselves is synonymous with accepting ourselves. Often it is easier to love and accept someone else then to really love and accept ourselves. But can we fully love and accept someone else when we lack love and acceptance of ourselves?

A few years ago, I attended a seminar in which we had to pair up with a partner for a specific exercise. I partnered with a woman I knew on a very casual basis. For the first part of the exercise, I was to look directly into her eyes and tell her how amazing she is and how loved she is. Then she would reciprocate by telling me how amazing and loved I was.

What I realized from this exercise was that it was *easy* for me to tell her how great and how loved she was. But I had a hard time *receiving* the love she was giving me.

I even teared up a couple of times and had to break eye contact. It was easy for me to give love to another person, but it was hard to *accept* love.

The reason it was hard for me to accept love was because I didn't fully love myself. I had low self-worth. This was evident in looking at the patterns of all my previous relationships. I had formed all of them based on a lack of love for myself.

This pattern even came up in financial and business situations. It was easy for me to give: free products, my time, and other things; but it was hard for me to accept anything—even money for products I had created and spent a great deal of time on. Anything I would receive, I would push away.

So my lack of self-love played out in my relationships, my work, and my finances. It wasn't until I fully learned to love myself that I manifested a loving relationship, loving friendships, and abundance.

So you can see that loving ourselves is very important to creating loving relationships, loving environments, and a loving world.

But the question is how do we really love ourselves?

First, ask yourself this question? What qualities do you look for in a romantic partner? Take a moment to think about them or write them down.

Now ask yourself; do you possess these same qualities? Most likely you do.

Next, what qualities do you possess that someone would like about you? Take a moment to think about them or write them down.

Remember that just as you can feel great love for someone else with certain qualities, that you possess those same qualities that make you lovable as well.

See for the longest time, I thought everyone else was worthy of love, except myself. But when I started realizing that I possessed those same qualities that I could fall in love with in someone else, I started loving myself.

It's a wonderful practice to fall in love with yourself. Granted there is a deeper, unconditional type of love beyond the feeling of being "in love"—which is often equated with "crushes" or "puppy love." But these feelings can point us to the deeper truth of ourselves—that we are pure love.

Practice Being In Love with Yourself

Have you ever been in love? You know—the feeling that love is in the air and everything around you is just vibrant and beautiful? The birds are singing, you are singing, you are walking around on a cloud, you can't wait to talk to that person, and you think about the person all the time. You smile more or maybe you're friendlier to those around you.

Well, what if we practiced being in love with ourselves? Now I'm not talking about having an ego and standing in front of the mirror for hours gawking at ourselves. But what if we really practiced being in love with ourselves?

In the past, I went through one of those lonely phases when I felt as if everyone had someone except me. Have you ever felt like that?

I really longed for that special connection with a romantic partner. Don't get me wrong, I did appreciate my girlfriends; but, for me, a connection with that special someone in an intimate relationship just can't be surpassed.

Then I thought back to times when I thought I was in love. I remembered the blissful beginnings of a relationship when we would dance in the rain, build sandcastles, play together, have tickle fests, drink champagne.

Recalling these memories made my heart race, and I felt the giddiness of a schoolgirl once again.

Then I asked myself a question. How am I different when I'm in love compared to how I am now, when I'm alone, lonely, and not in a relationship?

This is the answer that immediately entered my head: "When I'm in love I'm much more playful, more spontaneous. I sing more. I'm fun to be around."

Then I thought, "Could I be like that when I'm not in a relationship, when I'm not in love?" Could

Loving Yourself

I recreate that feeling of being in love and therefore recreate those actions?

I went back to the imagery of being in love. I really got in the moment. I began to feel light hearted and playful, like a wide-eyed kid. I felt my heart open up. I felt more joyful. I sang that Dean Martin song "When the moon hits your eyes like a big pizza pie, that's amore . . ." while dancing around my apartment.

Then I decided to drive to the beach for the day by myself. I played in the sand, I read a book, I took myself to dinner, and I played a couple of video games at a casino on the way home. I had a wonderful time, by myself.

The experience just proved to me that I could act as if I was in love and really feel and exhibit the qualities I did when I was in love even if I wasn't in a relationship.

This proved to me that it wasn't necessarily the person (the external), but the feeling (internal) that I longed for. I also realized that I could create that feeling myself. It wasn't dependent on anyone else.

From that experience, I also realized that I love the part of myself that's silly and light. I really like it when I'm playful, when I sing in public, when I dance and act silly. That's someone I could fall in love with. That someone is me.

There were times when I felt as if I could see myself through someone else's eyes—someone who really admired the fact that I built sandcastles.

Someone who thought it was cute when I sang off key and sang the same verses over and over. And that someone was me.

(And ironically, I attracted and married a man who really does think it's cute when I sing off key!)

Practice being in love with yourself. Recall a time when you were completely in love. (If you're in a relationship, recall the time when you first met.) Recall how you felt, how you acted, what you did. How were you different?

Bring that experience of being in love back into your reality and act the way you did then. Fall in love with yourself. Admire all those wonderful qualities about you.

What qualities did you fall in love with in your spouse or a previous partner? Do you possess those same qualities?

Most likely you do, and you can fall in love with those qualities in you. This will lead you to the deeper recognition of the pure love that you are.

Chapter 35

Loving Your Body

The increase in eating disorders and plastic surgeries indicates a widespread lack of love for our physical bodies.

Many of us do not like our bodies; thus we do not like ourselves. How can we love ourselves when we loathe our bodies?

Yet, we *all* have physical attributes we think are unlovable. We've heard even the most physically gorgeous models on television saying that they don't like some part of their physical makeup. One model says her thighs are too big. Another says her legs are too skinny and look like chicken legs.

Maybe we're too thin, maybe we're too big, maybe we're too flat chested, maybe we have a big butt or thighs, or maybe we have no butt. Whatever it is, most of us are not pleased with our physical bodies.

Can we learn to love those parts of our physical bodies that we feel are unlovable? Or love those parts of us that we don't like or wish we could change?

I haven't liked several things about my physical body. I've always disliked my hair. It is baby fine and thin. It's always been that way; it's in my genes. My hair would never grow past my shoulders, and there was absolutely nothing I could do about it.

Yet, I've heard of people who have beautiful, curly, wavy hair wishing it was straight, and vice versa.

I used to look enviously at women with long flowing hair. I would have given anything to have long, thick hair. I felt cursed for having thin hair. And beware my wrath toward the guy who would comment on the thinness of my hair or ask why I didn't grow it out.

Then one day when I went to the hairdresser, he said, "Your hair is so easy to style. It just stays where you place it." He added, "Be thankful you don't have to contend with the hassle of long, thick hair that doesn't stay in place."

Could the same quality that I've disliked so much for years be a blessing?

Find something loveable about a physical characteristic you haven't liked in yourself. I mentally listed all the benefits of having fine hair: It doesn't take long to dry, and when I apply hairspray, it stays in place.

Another area of my body that I never liked was my tummy. It's always been plump. I call it my poncha, like a kangaroo's pouch. No matter how skinny I was, I always had a plump round belly. I used to do abdominal exercises like crazy and nothing would change. Oh, I disliked my belly.

My husband sometimes rubs my belly and I get upset with him, thinking he's mocking me. But he says, "I think it's cute."

Cute? My belly? Can I look at my belly through his eyes, as being cute? Well, after all it is kind of cute . . . like a fluffy teddy bear . . .

Maybe it's your nose. Can you love your nose for giving you that unique look? Or maybe it's your entire physique. Can you love your physique for being the shape it is? Below are a couple of practices that can help you learn to love and respect your body.

Practices for Loving your Body

A while back, I saw a movie about spirituality titled *What the Bleep Do We Know?* (for more info, go to *www.whatthebleep.com*). In one scene, the main character takes an eyeliner pencil and draws hearts all over her body as a way of really loving herself. I thought it was neat. She was appreciating her body as a piece of art.

So I did this, and it was a phenomenal experience. With an old eyeliner pencil I wrote, "I am love," "I am sexy," "I love myself." I wrote these words on my stomach, my chest, my legs, my arms. I also decorated my body with hearts. Then I looked at myself in the mirror with love. It was such a great experience. Next time I'd like to get actual body paint. Look out!

So get out that old blue or purple eyeliner pencil that you never use, put on some joyful music, create affirmations, and write them on your body. It may sound weird, but it's fun. It's a loving thing to do.

Or, if you don't feel comfortable writing on your body, another helpful technique is to draw an outline of your body on a piece of paper.

See if there are any areas that you don't feel satisfied with, and color those areas with your favorite colors. Add some other colors to those areas that you really like about yourself. Then look at the drawing of you.

Look at all the wonderful colors of your body. Look at the beautiful rainbow of color that makes up *you*. You can also add affirmations to the drawing, such as "I love this package that my Spirit resides in." Have fun and practice loving your body.

Finally, another helpful exercise is to give thanks for your body. Know that your body is a shell that houses your wonderful Spirit. Be kind to your body. Thank it for being the vehicle that drives your Spirit.

My chiropractor brought it to my awareness that I was cursing my body. I used to say things like, "I can't believe I have allergies, most normal people don't have allergies," or "My body feels so old with all this back pain."

Instead, I started giving thanks for my body. I did a meditation where I just said thank you, over and over, to my body.

Thank you for being alive. Thank you for being the vehicle for me to walk around in. Thank you for being the house for my Spirit to reside in. Thank you for my uniqueness. Thank you.

Giving thanks is a powerful way to acceptance and love.

Chapter 36
Relationships as Mirrors

From the above chapter title, you might think that this subject should fall under part four: *How to Stop Hurting Others with Your Rubber Band*, but in fact, relationships serve as mirrors pointing out the things that we need to work on within ourselves.

As you've probably noticed by now, my past dating life has provided me ample opportunities to look at my values and beliefs, and most importantly, my beliefs about *myself* and not the other person.

It's easy to blame the other person for our bad relationships. It's easier to say, "Nothing's wrong with me; it's them."

But I've learned that relationships are mirrors to the way we feel about ourselves. I've also learned that the way people treat you indicates the way you see yourself.

If someone is treating you poorly, what inside you believes that you deserve to be treated poorly? If someone is judging you, what inside you feels a need to judge them or others?

I mentioned earlier that I have been alone for longer periods of time than I have been with someone. So I am a pretty independent person. I have a great network of friends and support, and I have a lot of side activities to keep me busy.

Before I met my husband, one guy I had been dating called me needy during one of our disagreements. This really triggered my Imposter and *it* came out in full force.

"I am far from needy," I thought to myself. "I am a risk taker. I have moved places by myself." I went on and on, defending myself.

But later I had to really look at *why* that comment had rubbed me the wrong way. That comment haunted me and bothered me for days. It triggered anger in me.

If I was so upset that I was judged as needy, did I posses that quality? Did I not like being called needy because I really was needy? The thought gave me the creeps.

Yet when I thought about my situation with this guy, it was clear that he was the gorgeous confident man who could have any woman, and I was the one *lucky* to be with him. So in a way, I had this energy of trying to get him to be attracted to me. Talk about needy.

Wow, this was a mirror held right up to my face, and I didn't like what I saw. The more I thought about it, the more I recognized that I did possess needy qualities. Yet I had adamantly denied those feelings or qualities. In fact, I had often gone to the other extreme by being so independent.

Remember I mentioned earlier that what you resist persists? Well, I had to realize that by not honoring those needy aspects of me, they would continue to show up in my relationships.

At the time, I was reading some material by relationship experts Gay and Kathleen Hendricks in which they talked about loving those parts of yourself that you feel are unlovable.

So I repeated this affirmation to myself: "I love that needy part of me." *Yikes.* I just couldn't love that part of me. I kept having a reaction to that affirmation.

So then I tweaked the affirmation to say, "I love the needy part of me that is really only desiring love." Okay, I could love that part of myself. We all want love.

That's when it hit me—my neediness was just a deep desire for love. That's a great quality to possess—to be so open and vulnerable to love.

As I repeated the above affirmation, I felt my body have less and less of a reaction toward the thought of being needy.

Ironically, after loving this needy part of myself, I didn't feel needy anymore. I loved that part of me that was wanting love, and through that love came the freedom from repeating past patterns.

I realized that this pattern kept showing up in order to be loved, to be honored, to be healed. When I gave it that love, it no longer had to express itself.

When I told my husband of my past neediness, he could hardly believe it because those dynamics don't play out in our relationship. In our relationship, both of us are very independent and interdependent. We love one another but don't feel a need to try to earn love or to get each other's love.

Though I admit that there are some moments in our relationship where I feel needy, but just by noticing it and accepting it, it doesn't have control over me or our relationship.

Are there any parts of you that you feel are unlovable? Can you love those parts?

If you're having a hard time loving those parts, can you do what I did and love yourself for expressing that quality as a desire for love?

If you can't love those parts of yourself that you feel are unlovable, can you love yourself for not loving those parts?

It's all about the love. Whenever something creeps up in us that isn't love, it is an area of ourselves that is calling for love.

By denying its existence or by resisting it, we empower it. By accepting it and loving ourselves, we diffuse its energy.

Next, we're going to discuss expressing ourselves.

Chapter 37
Dormant Dreams

His name was Mr. Green Jeans. At least that's what I called him. He was my sixth grade English teacher. He was 6'4" tall with an Afro hairdo, and he always wore green jeans. He looked like the Jolly Green Giant.

One day he read Edgar Allen Poe's "The Raven" to our class. Poe's writing, along with my teacher's deep voice and inflection, literally made the hair on my arms stand up. I had chills up and down my body.

I remember thinking to myself, "Wow, to be able to evoke such emotion through words." I decided I wanted to do that. I wanted to write a story that would make people *feel*.

I stayed up late at night for weeks writing a story about a little boy with leukemia. I researched the symptoms in my father's medical encyclopedia, and I typed up the story on my father's typewriter.

Then the day came to show my first novel to Mr. Green Jeans. I don't even remember its title, but I remember beaming with anticipation as I handed it to him. It was about fifty pages and was hole-punched, with a ribbon delicately holding it together.

He was delighted that I had written a story and said he couldn't wait to read it.

The next day he caught me after class and told me that he had read my book. He said I was quite talented, and that one day I would be a best-selling author.

I don't really know why I abandoned the possibility of a career in writing. And I don't know why I had forgotten this experience until a few years ago when someone asked me if I'd always wanted to be a writer.

I guess the ways of the world, adolescence, college, and reality all played a role in my decision to pursue a career in medicine. I knew I'd make good money; I knew I'd be self-sufficient.

I worked in the medical field for seven years before I quit my career to pursue my passion for writing. Medicine wasn't my passion, but it gave me security. It gave me independence. But the stress and the lie started taking a toll on me emotionally, spiritually, and physically.

I longed to write. I wanted to create stories. I had ideas for many stories, but by the time the work day was over and the responsibilities of my job were finished, I had no energy or creativity to write. I thought about changing careers often during those seven years. But I was too stable; I had put in too much time and schooling to turn back now. This is what I always told myself, anyway.

Then one day I had an experience that let me know I *had* to get out. The receptionist at the hospital where I was working was getting ready to leave early. It was about three in the afternoon, and I saw her packing her bag.

"You're lucky; you get to leave early," I said.

"Not really. I'm going to the dentist to have a tooth pulled," she said.

"I'd still rather go to the dentist and have a tooth pulled than stay here," I thought to myself.

Now normally, I would rather go anywhere but the dentist's office. The gynecologist didn't even bother me; but the dentist, yikes!

When I knew I'd rather go to the dentist than do what I was doing, I realized I was not living my heart's desire. I didn't feel it would be long before my body would be saying, "I'd rather die than continue doing this."

Part of me had already died inside. When you're given a gift, a talent, or a passion and you aren't expressing it, it's like snuffing out a candle. The candle wants to burn brightly. The candle has the flame (the desire), and yet you keep putting it out.

Several weeks later, in June 2001, I just up and quit my job in medicine. I quit my job like smokers who quit smoking cold turkey. One day they smoke, and the next day the ash trays are gone and they're done with it.

I decided to give myself six months to work on a novel I had been writing, off and on, for the last few years. If I didn't finish it and make it a success, I'd accept that I had tried and I'd go back to medicine.

I was working on my novel and another creative project when the tragedy of September 11th happened. Like many others, I was deeply concerned and in pain about the events. I found myself asking questions such as "How did we create a climate in which such things happen?" and "How can we move beyond hatred and violence to peace and love?" It was then that the idea for the book *Peaceful Earth* came to mind. I figured I would go to my spiritual mentors—all the authors I had studied—and seek their answers and then put those answers into a book.

It took me two full months of full-time effort to compile the book. And I had it published by December 2001. And here I am, still writing as well as speaking and exploring another passion of mine—screenwriting.

I absolutely know that if I had *not* created the space or the opening to be available to my passion for writing, the book *Peaceful Earth* would not have happened. And this book also would not have happened.

Had I still been working in medicine and received any of these ideas, I would not have had the time or energy or availability to pull it off.

And though I quit my job to work on a novel and another creative project, I was still available to redirect my energy toward a nonfiction book and to *act* when it was necessary.

I took a leap of faith in one direction, and the current took me in another direction. Sometimes we know what our passion is but we don't know exactly *how* it will express itself.

To me, this is what experiencing inner peace is really about: following your passion, pursuing your talent, honoring your God-given gift or talent, and then being open to the fact that you don't always know exactly how the expression of your talent will look.

Chapter 38
The Most Natural Thing

Off the top of your head, what is something that comes very naturally for you? Quickly say your answer out loud or write it down on a piece of paper.

What was your answer? Was it love? Was it painting? Was it taking care of children? Was it home repair work? Was it playing the drums? Was it crunching numbers or making calculations?

I believe that we all have an inherent gift, talent, or skill—something that is inherently easy and natural for us. The most natural thing for me is writing. I can easily and effortlessly sit down and type a ten-page document usually in less than an hour, whereas it takes some people hours or days to finish just a one-page letter or report.

Just the other day I sat down and whipped out a three-page letter within fifteen minutes. People who read the letter said it was very organized, well written, and beautiful. Many commented that it would have taken them hours to finish the same letter and that it wouldn't have been as clear.

At the same time, I struggle with accounting. But my friend Lynda can pop out my tax forms (both business and personal) in under an hour. She remembers numbers even if she has only heard them once. She's a genius with numbers.

My husband can play the drums to absolutely any song even if he's never heard it before. He doesn't have to read the music. He just starts playing once he hears the vocals or the other instruments, and it sounds amazing—as if he had practiced that song for hours. I can't even tap my fingers melodically. And don't ask me to sing; that's even worse.

We all know people who have a natural ability with children—kids just seem flock to them. And we also know people who have a knack for organizing or making home improvements. Many people have a natural ability to create—a piece of art, a song, a building, an outfit, a business, or an invention.

I believe that part of our purpose in life is to find out what our gift is and then to give it to others. It reminds me of a quote I read once by a man named Steve Bow; it went something like this: "God's gift to you is more talent, skill, and passion than you can ever imagine; your gift back to God is to use it."

You were endowed with a talent or natural ability for a reason. There are no accidents.

Think for a moment about your natural ability—the one you said out loud or wrote down in answer to my question at the beginning of this chapter. Is there any way you could use that gift to earn money? Or to make a career or occupation out of it?

Let's say you are one of the people who have a natural ability with children. Could you start a daycare center? Could you become a teacher? Or what if you have a green thumb? Could you become a florist or a landscaper?

The Most Natural Thing

I believe that when we do what comes naturally for us, the Universe supports us in terms of finances, connections, and resources.

Sometimes it's scary to make a step toward doing what comes naturally. Maybe you have a natural ability to create, but you've been working at a desk job for ten years and wouldn't know how to make the change. Start small. Create some arts and crafts and start selling it at craft fairs on the weekend. Make jewelry for your friends. If you follow your heart and do what you love, one day you'll be able to quit that desk job and make jewelry for a living.

If one person can make a living doing what he loves—anyone can. People are doing it everywhere, all the time. Tiger Woods makes a whole lot of money from doing what he loves and what comes naturally to him. Granted, I'm sure he's had some lessons and learned a lot along the way.

We've seen singers and musicians everywhere who have great careers and are doing what they love. We've seen people who love cooking open their own restaurants and enjoy success.

Find out what comes naturally to you and start incorporating it into your life. If part of what comes naturally to you is love, maybe you want to start a family or volunteer for the Peace Corps and spread love in a big way. Or maybe you want to become a mentor or teacher to spread love to others.

The possibilities are endless. Think about what comes naturally to you—and do it. It's an absolute disservice to humanity *not* to express your God-given talent.

Chapter 39
Passion

The root of the word "passion," *passio*, actually means "suffering" or "being acted upon." The most common meaning of passion is "an emotion that is deeply stirring or ungovernable."

So passion, really, is that driving force that propels us to put an end to the suffering of showing up as *less* than who we really are, and compels us to pursue something with *great* intensity.

Passion drives us to pursue our calling no matter what the cost. It is that inescapable, unavoidable desire to express ourselves. Passion defies rationality, in the sense that when you're passionate about something, you become it. It overtakes you. You are no longer being guided by the small voice in your head but by an urging for a deeper connection, a greater expression.

Passion is Spirit nudging you to step up to the plate; to live the life of joy, peace, abundance, vibrant health, expression, and expansion.

The driving force behind passion is *love*. What do you love? Who do you love? I remember a line from the movie *Adaptation*, with Nicolas Cage, that went something like this: "You are what you are passionate about."

Meryl Streep played a character who deeply wanted to be passionate about something. She wanted to know what it was like to feel strongly about something and to be compelled to pursue something which seemed larger than life itself.

People want more passion in their lives and in their relationships. Something inside of us yearns for greater expression, yearns to express love fully. Something inside us knows that we are meant to live in complete love and complete bliss—something inside us won't accept anything less.

Just as I asked previously about what came naturally to you, now I ask you to look at what your heart, your internal compass, longs for.

Sometimes people say they don't know what they want or they don't know what they are called to do.

Well, what do you love so much that you get lost in it? What gives you life?

And what if each of us could turn our passion into a career? What if each of us could experience the passion of our very first kiss on an ongoing basis in our current relationship? What if each of us could experience the passion of a child holding his or her first puppy or kitten? What about the passion of creating a piece of art, a marvelous dinner, or a deep, intriguing conversation?

I mentioned earlier that you *are* what you are passionate about. While passion catapults you into greater expression by driving you to pursue your deepest longing, you *are* your deepest longing.

You *are* your greatest desire. You *are* love personified. Your *passions* reveal the truth of who you *are*.

Passion

Passion is your internal guidance system; it is Spirit speaking through you to claim that which you desire. What you desire wants you. What you are passionate about wants you.

The only question is: will you follow that passion, that internal guidance which is urging you to express yourself in the most loving, most miraculous, grandest way? Passion is speaking through you now. What is it saying?

This is what passion says to me: live fully, enjoy every moment, love big, and express yourself.

Chapter 40
Right Before the Miracle

Sometimes we follow our passions but it seems as if we're not getting anywhere or that we won't be able to pursue them anymore.

I know that this feeling has overcome me numerous times while pursuing my passion. This is the feeling of trying to *make* something happen that I discussed in part two.

I also know that every time it seemed as if I was up against a wall or not getting anywhere, something happened to keep me going. I would get an E-mail from a person in Africa saying what a difference my words made to him, or I would get a check for the purchase of my book.

One time I was really questioning my life's purpose, wondering if I was doing the right thing because nothing seemed to be working out, when my friend Julianna invited me over.

She thought it might be nice to just forget about everything and spend some quality time together. In fact, she was house sitting for some friends who lived out in the country, and she thought it might be nice to spend time together there in the quietness of the country. (This is another example of not fighting what's going on but instead taking a break and allowing yourself to regroup and go with the flow.)

She gave me directions to the house. I was to get off the freeway, drive for about ten miles until I saw a Fred Meyer store on the right, and then turn right.

I got off the freeway and drove and drove. I kept looking for the Fred Meyer store on the right. I didn't see it. I continued to drive, still searching for that store.

I continued to drive until I thought I was actually leaving the city. I just knew I had driven more than ten miles, although I hadn't checked my odometer. Driving through a remote location, I knew I had gone too far. I knew I must have passed it.

So I turned around and retraced my route. I looked for the store, which would now be on my left. I continued keeping my eye out for the store.

Before I knew it, I was back at the freeway, where I had originally exited. Again I turned around and kept looking for the Fred Meyer store. I approached that same remote location and panicked. "I must have passed it again!"

Feeling lost, I called Julianna from my cell phone. She asked me what cross street I was at. I looked around and read the street name to her. She said, "Oh, you're not too far. Keep going, and you'll see it on the right." Reassured, I got off the phone with her.

Just then, I noticed the huge Fred Meyer sign one block ahead. It was only a block away from the location where I had previously turned around.

Seeing the store right there in clear sight, knowing it had been only one block away from the point I had turned around, made me wonder: what if we knew that our dream or goal was only moments from being achieved?

Sometimes it feels as if we continue to pursue our dreams, day after day, night after night; and we feel as if we aren't getting anywhere or as if nothing's happening; and so we decide to give up.

But what if we knew that the dream or miracle was only one more day away or one more block away? What if we knew it was figuratively right around the corner?

Yet when we don't see it, many of us get frustrated, thinking that it will never happen. We give up or change course, when the goal is within arm's reach (or driving range.)

Remember that saying, "God can see around corners, but we can't." If we knew that the thing we were searching for was right around the corner, would we turn around? Most of us wouldn't.

And yet in reality, that's what most of us do. Most of us live our daily lives needing to see the results of our labor, requesting a guarantee that something will work before we try it.

When you feel like giving up, know that the miracle is right there. If you can surrender to the moment, you can uncover the miracle.

I once heard a saying that the Universe doesn't give you a dream, a hunch, or an idea without giving you the *way* to achieve it. The *way* is there, but sometimes we don't see it even though it's right in front of our eyes!

Chapter 41
Fear of Failure and Rejection

Until now we have been exploring the topics of living from the inside out, accepting yourself and expressing yourself. But many other topics also fall under the category of how we hurt ourselves with our rubber bands (i.e., our experiences).

Most of us experience fear of failure and rejection, worry over finances, and fear of death. Many of us also unintentionally use our language to hurt ourselves. And many of us hurt ourselves by continually looking outside for that expert advice. I will discuss all of these topics next, starting with the fear of failure and rejection.

I mentioned earlier that in my previous dating experiences I had encountered lots of rejections. But then I realized that the reason I encountered more rejections than most people was because I put myself out there more than most people.

Many of the people I knew hadn't encountered many rejections, but they hadn't had too many successes either. They pretty much settled or stayed in their comfort zone.

I have also experienced numerous rejections as a writer. But I take this as part of the process.

We need to look at rejections and failures differently. In Robert Kiyosaki's book *Rich Dad, Poor Dad,* he talks about investing in real estate. He mentions that out of one hundred houses you look at, maybe you'll find one or two great investments. That's a lot of duds compared to the good ones you find!

In one of Kiyosaki's books he mentions that Colonel Sanders was rejected one thousand times before he sold his famous Kentucky Fried Chicken recipe. One thousand times! Now if Colonel Sanders had looked at rejection as failure, he would have never been successful; he would have given up.

Sylvester Stallone was down and out, broke, and living out of his car with his dog. His wife left him because he refused to get a job; he knew if he got a job he would never sell his screenplay *Rocky*. At one time he was offered hundreds of thousands of dollars for his screenplay, if he would *not* act in it. He turned down the offer because he knew in his heart he was supposed to act in it. And we all know the success of the movie *Rocky*. It catapulted Stallone's career to the next level. And five sequels have been made.

We need to change our thinking in regard to rejection and failures. We need to look at failures as learning experiences, opportunities for growth. And instead of fearing rejection, we need to remember that whatever is meant to happen will happen. We must trust the Universe to unfold as it should.

Again, it's remembering that good and bad are relative. A failure may turn out to be our greatest success. A rejection may really be our greatest blessing.

Chapter 42
Worry over Finances

I know about financial worries all too well, ever since I quit a lucrative career in medicine to pursue my passion for writing.

Since then, I have been fraught with financial struggle and worry most of the time.

I have been in panic mode many times, wondering how I would even pay rent. I've sold anything I could just to get by.

It's not a good feeling when you're riddled with worry and fear over finances. Yet most of us worry about finances daily. In fact, many of us live month to month, struggling to get by.

There are many books out there on abundance and prosperity, and I encourage you to spend some time reading books on this topic.

Something that made an important difference for me was the realization that I had been using affirmations incorrectly.

"I need to manifest abundance, so that I can continue doing what I am doing," I would say to myself. And I made a strong commitment to really focus—by way of affirmations and visualizations—on attracting and manifesting abundance in my life so that I could continue pursuing my writing and speaking career.

One of my affirmations was "Money and circumstances easily and effortlessly flow to me."

Then I would vividly picture money flowing to me, easily and effortlessly. What's wrong with this picture?

I realized that I had it all backwards. Instead of money flowing to me, it really flows through me, if I would just allow it to happen.

The mere affirmation that money *flows to me* implies that I do not have money. That I am in a state of lack—a state of being without.

The very thing that I was trying to draw to me, I was actually repelling by focusing my energy on the lack.

As I mentioned earlier, quantum physics tells us that the world is but a reflection of what we see or what we believe. If you see and know and believe abundance, you create that reality for yourself. When you affirm lack, you experience lack.

I know these spiritual truths from my years of studying spirituality, but I hadn't realized that by the simple affirmation and visualization of money flowing to me, I was affirming and concentrating on the lack of money in my life.

Okay, so how could I get to the point of being able to affirm that abundance is flowing through me when I really don't see any money, and I don't have money to pay my bills?

In his book *The Infinite Way,* Joel Goldsmith demonstrates the law of supply using an example of an orange tree.

Think about an orange tree right now. What does an orange tree do? Produce oranges. But what about the times when the orange tree is not producing oranges? Do we doubt that it will ever produce oranges?

No, we're pretty sure that even though we don't see oranges at the moment, the orange tree will produce oranges. What if we looked at our financial situations in the same way?

Goldsmith says, "The orange is the result or effect of the operation of the law (law of nature, law of supply) acting in, through, and as the orange tree. As long as this law is present we will have oranges."

In this example we can see that the oranges (the fruit) represent the effects of the supply but the supply is actually the tree. So the oranges are the effects and the tree is the supply.

Many of us erroneously think that the oranges are the supply. But once they are picked or fall off the tree, new oranges start to grow. If the oranges were the supply, when they were gone, there would be no new oranges. The oranges, like money, are the *effect* of the law of supply.

The tree, which is the supply, is actually working through its root systems to produce more oranges. The law of supply is always in effect, continually working through the tree to produce more oranges. Just as the law of supply is working through us.

Goldsmith says, "Let us learn to think of dollars, as we do of leaves on trees or oranges, as the natural and inevitable result of the law active within."

Goldsmith reminds us not to worry when the tree seems bare, because the law is operating within it to bring forth fruit.

Money is also an effect. Money is energy.

So instead of using the affirmation, money easily flows to me, I use "money is flowing through me. The law of supply is always providing."

We are like the orange tree in the sense that we inherently have all that we need or desire within us. We only need to *allow* it to express through us as our consciousness.

A powerful affirmation and visualization that I use now if I start to fret about finances is this:

I visualize the orange tree. I visualize myself as the orange tree. I affirm that the law of the Universe is consistently working through me to express my highest good. I affirm that even though I may not see abundance, I know that the law of supply is working through me to produce exactly what I need for my ultimate expression.

When I am able to be in this place of knowing and trusting in the abundance of the Universe, it supplies me with all that I need.

I have experienced this so many times when I thought I was lacking and then affirmed the truth. I would then receive a refund check in the mail, a gift from a parent, or some other form of unexpected income. And I have been able to sustain myself for the last five years, doing what I love.

I would like to end this chapter with a final quote from Joel Goldsmith:

"All of the good necessary to our welfare will be supplied to us in greater abundance than we can accept when we give up the effort and desire to get, achieve, or accomplish, and come more into the consciousness of desiring only to fulfill our destiny on earth. We are Consciousness fulfilling and expressing Itself in an individual way, and if we will learn to keep our thought away from ourselves and away from the fear that we will be without place or income or health, and let God fulfill Its destiny through us or as us, we will really find all things added unto us."

I had realized an important distinction that enabled me to shift from trying to draw circumstances to me to just allowing things to unfold through me.

Money is energy. And abundance is everywhere. We only have to look up at the stars in the sky to see the abundance of the Universe.

If we are not experiencing abundance, then we have cut ourselves off from the law of supply through our thoughts of lack or our worries over finances.

If you are not experiencing financial abundance, look at your predominant thoughts and emotions. We impede the natural flow of life with thoughts of lack and worry.

Elevate your vision to see beyond an orange tree with no oranges, and to see the law of supply always working through you and available to you at any moment.

Chapter 43
Fear of Death

It has been documented that one of our greatest fears is fear of death. I talked about how I used a Buddhist meditation of contemplating death as a way to help ease my fear. Even so, that fear lingered with me on and off for quite some time.

But when I was face to face with the death of both of my cats, within the last few years, I have looked at life and death differently.

I had heard it said that it is a sacred act to be with someone as he or she makes the transition. I was present when both of my cats passed away. Now anyone who has ever had a pet knows how they are part of the family. Tigger was 17 when he died a few years ago and Talmage was 17 when he died a month prior to completion of this book.

Tigger died naturally at home, and Talmage was "put to rest" because his kidneys were failing. I tried to let him pass away naturally, but decided to have a veterinarian come to our home and euthanize him when he stopped eating and drinking and appeared to be suffering.

I have no judgment or comment on the two processes—dying a natural death or euthanasia. However, I know that I did what I felt was best for each of my companions based on each of their unique situations. I'm still grieving the loss of Talmage. I had him 17 years and he was my best friend. Though I miss him physically, I know he's with me.

One thing I learned from being present with both of my cats when they made their transition was that death is really just a transference of energy. If we are attached to bodies, then death is painful and sorrowful. But if we realize that we are more than our bodies, death takes on a new meaning.

I witnessed first hand that though the body disintegrates, the Spirit or energy of the animal or person remains. There is something that remains of us, even after our physical bodies have departed.

I believe we can still feel the energy of the animal or person that has died. Shortly after Tigger died, as I fell asleep in my recliner, I heard him purring. I've also experienced the sensation of him jumping on the bed. And one morning I heard him meow. It was his way of showing me that he will always be with me.

One time when I fell asleep, while really missing Tigger and wanting to pet him, he appeared to me in a dream.

He was lying in a pasture, with rolling green hills. He was basking in the sun. He looked like a tiger. Then I noticed there were two tigers, one on each side of him, resting in the grass as well. There was a fence separating Tigger and me, and I asked a person standing next to me if Tigger would be safe. Won't the tigers eat him? Should I go save him?

Fear of Death

The person said that Tigger would be safe and that the tigers would not eat him. That he was their family, and he was home.

I believe that I am still and always will be fully connected to Tigger beyond his animal body. And I know now that any time I call on him, he comes to comfort me.

Talmage has also visited me in dreams. And the dreams feel so real. I am petting him and he is purring. He is at peace, I am at peace. My cats are always with me.

During the editing of this book, my grandmother, Nina, passed away. Though we all adored Nina, and were deeply saddened, my mom was especially devastated. So I prayed for my mom, asking God to comfort her with the *knowing* that her mom is always with her.

A couple of weeks later, my mom called me and said she was shopping at a flea market and kept being drawn toward this particular potted plant. She kept circling it and looking at other things, until she decided to buy it. She took it home and was cleaning some of the dirt out of the pot, and on the inside of the pot it said "Nina."

My grandmother lived and died in Indiana, and my mother was shopping at a flea market in New Mexico. Plus how many people do you know named Nina?

That was even more confirmation to me that people don't die, they just change form. I know that we are more than our physical bodies. I know that there is an energy of us that remains after our physical bodies have departed.

If we believe we *are* our bodies, then we will fear death. We will fear losing our loved ones to death; we will fear dying ourselves. But if we know that we are more than our human bodies, and that from this perspective we never really die, then we open up to the greater truth. We are all eternal.

Energy is neither created nor destroyed. Know that if you have lost loved ones, you can still connect with them. Their energy is still with you. And they will always be a part of you.

Know also that when your physical body departs, the Essence of you will live on forever.

Chapter 44

Using Words as Weapons

Often, unintentionally, we hurt ourselves with the words we use. It is equivalent to snapping ourselves with a rubber band.

Remember that saying when you were little, "Sticks and stones can break my bones, but words can never hurt me"? Well, ironically, words can and do hurt us. Sometimes our words deliver shattering blows to ourselves or others, greater than any stick or stone ever could.

Entire fields, such as neurolinguistic programming (NLP), have been dedicated to the study of words and their effect on our results or experiences. But the most compelling studies have been done by a Japanese scientist Masaru Emoto, and they are revealed in his book *Messages from Water*.

Emoto has extensively studied and photographed water crystals under varying conditions. He exposed water to various words by writing them on the bottled water and then photographing the resultant water crystals. All the other variants were the same except for the word placed on the water bottle. The water that was exposed to words such as "love" or "thank you" showed beautiful, very complex, ornate water crystals. Water that was exposed to words such as "hate" or phrases like "I'm going to kill you" demonstrated no crystal structure or poorly defined crystalline structure. Emoto reminds us that our bodies are 70 percent water. If words do this to water, what are words doing to our bodies?

Advertisers have long recognized the ability of words to trigger associations and certain emotions.

I'd like to explore how we use words in our everyday life, often to the detriment of ourselves and others.

Words are the first act of creation. When we say something, or put it in writing, we are literally taking our thoughts or emotions and stamping them into a concrete reality.

Some of the words or phrases I'm going to talk about may be obvious; some may be words you hadn't even thought about, words you find yourself using in your daily life. I encourage you to take a look at the words you use, and choose your words carefully.

1) *Try*

How many of us have said things like "I'm going to try to lose weight" or "I'd like to try something different"?

The word "try" automatically gives us an escape route. "I'm going to try. . . ." but if I don't like it, or if I don't succeed. . . .

You either do it or you don't; you don't *try* to do it. So instead of saying "I'm going to try to lower my voice," why not eliminate the word "try" altogether and say, "I'm going to lower my voice."

2) You make me . . .

During a disagreement, how many of us have said to a partner or co-worker, "You make me so mad . . ." or "you make me feel . . ." When you say somebody or something makes you feel a certain way, you are taking responsibility off yourself and placing it outside yourself. No one can make you feel a certain way. You make yourself feel that way. No thing can make you feel hurt. You feel hurt. So instead of saying "You make me so mad when you do this," a more accurate phrase would be "I feel angry when this happens." Or, even more powerful, "I am choosing to feel this way."

3) God awful

Does anyone remember this slang term used to describe something miserable or absurd or downright ugly? Recently, I was making a joke about those God-awful hospital gowns that are open in the back. Then a friend of mine brought to my attention the fact that the words "God" and "awful" don't belong in the same sentence together. You can say the same about this slang phrase: Holy shit.

4) Filthy rich

How many of us have seen a movie star on television or someone driving in a limo and said that person is filthy rich? By combining the words "filthy" and "rich," we are saying that money is dirty. And, if we believe that money is dirty we will repel it.

5) *I can't believe it* . . .

Have you ever won a prize or received a bonus or some other exciting news and then said, "I can't believe it?" If we say something like this when something good happens, we are implying that we can't believe that the good happened. Or, that we can't believe that something good would happen *to us*. Winning prizes, getting raises, achieving a goal are natural parts of our lives. It is our divine birthright to receive and express all the forms of love in the Universe. When we use phrases like "I can't believe it," we invalidate that the love is part of our natural heritage.

6) *That just kills me; that makes me sick.*

How many of us have heard a funny joke or witnessed something really absurd and said, "That just kills me?" Or what about the phrase, "Go break a leg?" Do we really choose to manifest things like killing ourselves, making ourselves sick or breaking body parts?

7) *Want*

How many of us have said "I want a new car" or "I want some peace of mind." The word "want" has a sense of desperation to it. When you want something you usually first are saying that you do not have that item. In the Sedona Method, I learned to substitute the words "allow myself to have" in place of the word "want." So instead of saying "I want to buy that item" I now say, "I allow myself to buy that item." The latter statement is much more life affirming and active.

8) *Hope*

I "hope" that she gets the job or I "hope" that it all works out. This is another weak word that implies a sense of desperation. We could easily replace sentences like "I hope I get the job" with "I know that I will get the job if it is for my highest good and the highest good of the employer."

9) *Hate*

What is one of the worst four-letter words in our vocabulary? "Hate." "Hate" is a strong word with a strong emotion. How often do we use this word in our everyday conversation? I know I find myself saying things like "I hate it when my food gets cold." Yet our subconscious minds still have to go to that place of "hate" when we use the word. It can't tell the difference between hatred for another person and hatred of cold food. Since we are energetic beings creating our reality, we would benefit from avoiding use of words such as "hate." It's like that infomercial that says "hate" is a four-letter word, and so is "love." Which will you use?

10) *Not*

Neuro linguistic programming states that the subconscious mind is unable to recognize the word "not." So instead of "I'm not sick," your subconscious mind hears "I am sick." It's almost like saying "Don't think of pink elephants." What does your mind do? It thinks of pink elephants. It is wise to word things in the positive. So instead of saying "I am not sick," affirm the results you desire by saying, "I am healthy."

11) *Good luck*

I would like to come up with another phrase for this one. Really, there is no such thing as "luck," and from a higher perspective nothing is good or bad; it just is. What about a phrase like "Knowing your highest is unfolding . . ." This is rather lengthy. Can you think of a shorter phrase?

    I encourage you to think of other words or ways we use them that may not be producing the results we desire. If you have some you'd like to share with me, please E-mail them to *lisa@peacefulearth.com*.

    And remember: choose your words wisely.

Chapter 45
Seeking Expert Advice

Most of the material on success that I have read stresses the importance of having mentors—people who have already reached the exact place you want to be. Many of these mentors are considered to be experts in their particular fields.

While I believe in the idea of having mentors, there is a fine line between trying to be like another person (i.e., your mentor) and finding your own voice, perhaps under the guidance of a mentor.

For the longest time, I was trying to be the next Tony Robbins, Wayne Dyer, or other spiritual or self-help guru. I was trying to be everyone else but me. Little did I know I was setting myself up for disappointment.

Some of my so-called mentors turned out *not* to be who I thought they were. One of them got into legal trouble for money issues and another was rude and egotistical when I met him in person at one of his speaking engagements. (By the way, I am *not* speaking of either Tony Robbins or Wayne Dyer when I talk about the anonymous mentors above.)

Let's just say that after seeing them for who they really were, I was disillusioned, especially because I had spent years trying to be just like them. Now who could I look up to? Who could I emulate?

We tend to make mentors or experts out to be heroes or icons in our minds. We make them out to be something they are not. Even our heroes and icons have bad days. Even they sometimes have poor judgment. And as mentioned earlier, sometimes they can be rude even when they preach kindness.

The problem with making someone out to be so great is that when you find out they're just like the average Joe, it can be disillusioning. Especially if you've spent years trying to be like them. Talk about being crushed!

And sometimes you lose yourself trying to be someone else. My book *Peaceful Earth* was a compilation of stories and summaries from many of my spiritual mentors. I wanted to know what they would say about creating peace and love. In the book I included a small summary of my own thoughts, but it was mostly a compilation of great spiritual thinkers. And I hadn't considered myself to be one of them.

I spent a great portion of my life, devoted to marketing and spreading the messages of *their* wisdom.

One day, I got a call from Mike Gerdes, who has supported my work since day one. We reminisced about the book *Peaceful Earth.* Then he said, "I'd like to hear what Spirit says through Lisa instead of what other people say." And this book is entirely Spirit speaking through me.

When I put together *Peaceful Earth,* I didn't think I was an authority who could address the subject of peace or spirituality. I felt as if I needed an expert opinion. I also felt that I wasn't good enough to be heard or listened to, or that I didn't have anything

Seeking Expert Advice

important to say. I had to be "one of them" before people would pay attention to what I was saying.

Now I have found my own voice and my own path. And yes, I still read material from others and buy courses from others. But I don't feel that I need to be like them. I look at their material and then I decide what I take from it and what I don't.

We all have an inner expert and authority inside of us, and I think it's important to not be so focused on trying to be someone else but for each of us to find our unique inner expert and let that inner expert speak and be heard.

Granted, I have great friends and associations. I associate with people who possess some of the qualities I try to emulate. This way it's more of a support system instead of me trying to be someone else.

I prefer not to get into the role of expert and subject. Yet as a speaker, I know that question-and-answer sessions are important. They are a valuable form of exploration. But part of me is hesitant to do a question-and-answer format because it places me in a position of authority, as if I, or anyone else, has the answer for *you*.

I was once in that same situation asking the experts how to help *me* run *my* life.

So now I often preface my answers with the phrase "What has worked for me is . . ." Then I make sure to let questioners know that they need to discover on their own what works for them.

When any tragedy or unexplainable event would happen I used to ask myself, "I wonder what Eckhart Tolle would say about that" or "I wonder what Wayne Dyer's response would be?"

Now I go within and allow my own inner wisdom to express itself. Often during meditation, I'll just ask myself those same questions: "What does this experience mean?" or "How should I respond to this situation?" Then I allow that inner wisdom to guide me.

Find your inner mentor, your inner expert. Find your own path and your own voice. Yes, read and learn from others; but don't feel that you need to be like them. Learn from them and incorporate their teachings in your own way. Realize that they are human and that they were once in your exact spot, trying to find their own voices.

Create positive associations and support networks in which you all work together to support one another on your spiritual path. In your associations, no one is better than the other and no one is weaker than the other. Everyone just brings different things to the table.

And yes, I still believe mentoring is valuable, especially in certain situations. Say, for example, that I don't know anything about real estate, but I'd like to start buying homes. It would be valuable for me to find an expert on real estate and ask him or her questions or read his or her material. But then I'm going to trust my own inner expert on whether to act on the advice I receive.

Seeking Expert Advice

Again, I still recommend reading books on subjects of interest. Maybe the author will express something in a way that you haven't heard before, and maybe that new insight will help you. But at the same time, realize that you already inherently know the wisdom they speak of; maybe they just said it in a different way or used a different technique. A true mentor doesn't want to create clones but wants to help people find their own voice, their own path, and their own way.

I believe there's a proverb that says something like this: The best gift you can give a teacher is to *not* have to use him or her anymore.

Take notes, listen to ideas, learn new techniques, read material, and decide for yourself how you express that information.

All the genius, wisdom, and expertise is inside of you already. Don't try to be someone else. Find a way to express *you*.

Chapter 46
Playing the Martyr

According to Webster's Dictionary a martyr is "one who makes great sacrifices or suffers much in order to further a belief, cause, or principle".

Wayne Dyer at one of his seminars said something like this; "I can't get sick enough to heal the world." Can we get poor enough to heal the world of poverty?

Let's face it, we all love the martyr. That's what makes for good movies. And as a screenwriter, I know the power of using a martyr character to draw people into the story. We pay lots of money to see movies or read books about these types of heroes/heroines. These are the people we idolize; these are the people we look up to. The ones that were handed everything on a silver platter haven't earned our attention.

In fact, *Rudy* is still my favorite movie. Rudy is based on the real life story of Rudy Ruettiger who is a small guy that dreamed of playing football for Notre Dame. The struggles and obstacles he overcame to pursue his dream really tug at my heart.

I commend and respect anyone who has overcome great adversity. Yet, I also have to wonder how many of us *create* suffering in our own lives so that we can be the martyr?

I know that I have done this in my life. I have always aspired to be a writer because writing comes naturally to me. And I also know that all the writers who I have wanted to be like, have shared stories of severe struggles against adversity.

Sylvester Stallone was broke and had a failed marriage before he finally sold *Rocky*. I can't tell you the number of authors I have heard of who have gone through a bankruptcy. Many authors also grew up in poverty. They all had a *story* that they had to rise above.

Somehow, subconsciously, I believed that I had to be a martyr. That I had to struggle and overcome adversity in order to be successful. In order to be a famous writer I had to have a down-and-out story.

So, sure enough I quit my job to pursue my passion for writing. I went broke. I ate Top Ramen because it was the only thing I could afford. I lived in dread wondering how I would pay my bills. I went bankrupt. I struggled and I suffered all in the name of pursuing my dream. I was the martyr.

Now I was just like all the authors who went from a struggling writer to successful author. I now had my story. And while I was one step closer to being just like my mentors with their down and out stories, I can tell you that this is no way to live.

Can we have the success stories without the suffering? I choose to believe so.

And how many of us have played the martyr in our relationships?

I know I've been in relationships with alcoholics and pot heads, thinking I could save them. I've been in relationships with abusive men thinking I could change them. I've been in relationships with

Playing the Martyr

angry men thinking I could help them.

In fact, while in a spiritual Practitioner program I've heard women in emotionally abusive relationships say they were going to stay in the relationship because it was their duty to be more spiritual and learn how to be peaceful despite their partner's destructive patterns. And believe me, I've done this as well.

I thought if I was more spiritual I should be able to stay in an abusive relationship and not allow it to affect me.

And while it's true that we have to shine the light of our consciousness into any situation, it doesn't mean we need to subject ourselves to abuse. Once you shine your consciousness into any unconscious relationship your partner will either become more conscious or the relationship will disintegrate naturally.

But to salvage the unconscious relationship once it is disintegrating to be *more spiritual* is ridiculous. You can lovingly let go of that person and lovingly release the relationship. You don't need to play the martyr anymore.

In all of the previous scenarios, the struggling writer and the codependent woman, I was suffering for the greater good. I was sacrificing my well being to save the man. I was sacrificing my joy to have a story to tell to help all the other struggling writers.

But am I really helping others by playing the martyr? Are any of us really helping others by playing the martyr?

Are there situations in your life where you've played the martyr? And if so, how can you have all that you desire without the suffering?

Once I realized I was playing the martyr, I realized that I could also choose a different role. None of us need to be martyrs in order to help others or in order to live our true purpose.

What if you could have all that you desire, without the suffering? What if that could be your story? What if that could be the legacy you leave to others?

Chapter 47
Gratitude

A very important way to stop hurting ourselves with our rubber bands (or experiences) is to continually give thanks for everything. In part four, I will discuss the power of giving thanks for people in your life, but in this chapter I'll focus on giving thanks for everything that happens in your life experience.

It goes back to the theory mentioned previously, that good and bad are relative. If we can get to the point where we can be thankful for *all* of our life experiences, we will suddenly realize the blessings all around us.

Have you noticed that we normally only give thanks for the things that are going right in our lives? How often do we give thanks for absolutely everything in our lives, even the situations that we deem negative or bad?

Around Thanksgiving every year I send out an article and a poem I wrote about "Giving Thanks for Everything" which is printed on the next page.

But it's important to consistently be thankful for everything every day, not just on Thanksgiving.

Giving Thanks for Everything

I am thankful not only for my successes, my friendships, my relationships, my health, and the material things in my life but for the difficulties, the challenges that ended up being opportunities for new growth.

I am thankful for the failed relationships that taught me true love.

For those financial challenges that forced me to analyze my priorities. For those brick walls that I felt up against, which taught me how to climb.

For those broken hearts that opened me up inside.

For those setbacks that showed me I was headed in the wrong direction.

For those rejections that taught me self-worth.

For those tears that showed how deeply I cared.

For losses incurred, which taught me that I never really "had" anything.

For the stress that told me to slow down.

For the fear of the unknown, which taught me how to live in the moment. For the doubt that brought me closer to God.

For the "dark night of the soul" that showed me the truth of who I am beyond my experiences.

For the pain that cracked me open. I am reminded of a quote that says, "What is death to the acorn is birth to the oak tree." I know that beyond

Gratitude

anything that we deem negative, bad, or painful, there is a peace, an opportunity, or a blessing.

I am thankful for all the experiences that are a natural part of being in this human body, for they continue to show me the truth of who I am beyond name and form.

I give thanks for endings, because I know that the ending of one thing is the beginning of something else. I give thanks for all the experiences or difficulties in life that connect me with that unalterable, unshakable peace of God inherent within. I give thanks for absolutely everything.

In summary, when we start living from the inside out, when we accept and express ourselves, and when we live in a state of gratitude, we no longer snap ourselves with our rubber bands. We no longer hurt ourselves, and we become free to be who we really are.

PART FOUR:

How to Stop Hurting Others with Your Rubber Band

Chapter 48
Realizing our Unity from a Bottle of Bubbles

I mentioned earlier that the key to inner peace is healing our sense of separation from our Source, and the key to world peace is healing our sense of separation from each other. This chapter is devoted to realizing our connectedness and dissolving our sense of separation. Any time we feel separate from others or judge others, it is as if we are shooting them with our rubber bands. We are literally hurting others.

Mother Teresa said, "If there is no peace, it is because we have forgotten that we belong to one another." Manifesting world peace involves declaring our unity and realizing that we are all one.

Many of us have heard the concept that we are all one, yet many of us have a hard time understanding it or grasping its meaning.

I like to use a bottle of bubbles as an analogy for our connectedness.

Picture holding a bottle of bubbles in your hand. Now picture using the wand to blow bubbles. Then picture all of the beautiful bubbles surrounding you.

Now imagine that one bubble represents you. Another bubble represents your spouse or partner, another represents a co-worker, another a public figure, and another a stranger.

Now notice where *all* the bubbles came from. They all came from the same bottle. They are all made up from the same liquid.

So in this analogy the liquid soap is the Source, and the bubbles are the multiple expressions. We are the multiple expressions of the one Source. At the most basic level, we are all connected. Notice I have used the word "Source" instead of "God." We'll explore that topic next in the chapter "Honoring All Beliefs."

I like to remember the bubble analogy any time I feel separate from someone. Remember that although you appear to be separate from another person, you are really made up of the same Source.

Yet, even though we all come from the same Source, many of us have different beliefs. In the next chapter, we will look at what a belief really is.

Chapter 49
~~Honoring all Beliefs~~

Most arguments and disagreements, and thus most acts of violence and war, stem from having different beliefs and trying to impose our beliefs on another person or group of people.

When we try to impose our beliefs on others, we are metaphorically shooting them with our rubber bands. Sadly, in the real world we are shooting people with weapons (guns and bombs) and using our words as weapons.

Here's what usually happens when you and a person have a different belief: Someone tries to convince you of his or her belief; then you try to convince him or her of your belief; then the other person tries harder to convince you of his or her belief; then you try harder; and finally you both walk away angry, nothing solved. Or you end up in a heated debate until you're blue in the face and then you vow never to see that person again because he or she is obviously wrong.

Or, in the worst-case scenarios, you try to enforce your beliefs on others by committing acts of violence, they retaliate, you recruit more people and get bigger weapons, they recruit more people and use different tactics, and a lot of people die in the process.

So how do we get to the point where we can honor all beliefs, not argue or defend our beliefs, and not have the need to impose our beliefs on others?

First, we have to take a look at what a "belief" really is. Webster defines a "belief" as "Something believed or accepted as true." The interesting thing about this definition is that what may be true for you may not be true for me. Our beliefs are based on our current reality and are really *values* based on our background, culture, upbringing, or personal preferences.

For example, I may have a belief that chocolate cake is the best dessert in the world. Now that does not make me right or wrong; that is just my belief.

On the other hand, you may have a belief that carrot cake is the best dessert in the world. Or you may have a belief that fruit is the best dessert in the world because it's the healthiest. Again, that doesn't make you right or wrong; it is just your belief.

Now you can show me all the studies and statistics in the world that prove that fruit is the best dessert, but you most likely will not get me to change my mind. Let's face it, I just like chocolate cake.

We can go back and forth and argue until we're both blue in the face, and you won't convince me that fruit is the best dessert and I won't convince you that chocolate cake is the best dessert.

Another definition of a belief is "Mental acceptance of and conviction in the truth, actuality, or validity of something." Again, you can see this demonstrated in the differing beliefs about the best dessert.

The most important thing to note is that beliefs are human constructs; they are mind based. And again they often depend on our upbringing, culture, or past. Because beliefs are of the mind, when you go up against someone with your belief you are engaging in a battle of the minds (or a battle of the egos). Does this solve anything?

To repeat what Einstein said, you can't solve a problem from the same level of thinking that created the problem. Arguing beliefs is meeting the problem (a mental construct) on the same level with another problem (mental construct). Beliefs are personal opinions (or collective opinions, as with religion, which we'll discuss shortly).

Any time you have a belief (a personal, mind-made opinion), there will *always* be someone who has another opinion or belief. If your group has certain beliefs, you will always encounter another group that has other beliefs.

So how do we move beyond the battle of the minds? The answer is to honor all beliefs. We must remind ourselves that at the level of belief we will always have differences, but that the differences aren't right or wrong; they just are.

Again, I prefer chocolate cake and I'm sure I have many who will agree with me that chocolate cake is the best. But that doesn't make the lovers of carrot cake wrong. It doesn't make the fruit lovers wrong.

As mentioned earlier, a belief is a mind-constructed reality based on personal preferences, background, or culture. In my mind, I think chocolate cake is the best dessert. That makes it real for me. But it may not be real for you.

For me to enjoy chocolate cake, do I have to make you like chocolate cake too? Do I have to be an enemy of all the fruit lovers?

These are important questions to start asking ourselves. If we do so, and we begin to honor *all* beliefs, we will create a climate that is peaceful and loving.

Chapter 50

Love Is My Religion

Throughout history, religious beliefs have been the cause of most arguments and feuds. Most acts of war and violence have resulted from differing religious beliefs.

Yet the world is big enough for all kinds of beliefs, and part of the process of peace-keeping is to honor different beliefs, including different religious beliefs.

Currently, there is much separation among religions. The followers of each religion believe they have a monopoly on God, and that their way is the only way. Each religion purports to be right.

People have reduced the infinite God to a human, mind-made construct—a name or a belief system. We have taken the infinite and made it finite.

Again, any time you reduce something to a level of belief you will always find someone who has an opposing belief.

The difference among many religions is in the name given to God, yet we are all really talking about the same being, presence, consciousness. The name we choose—God, Allah, Mother Earth, or Frank—does not matter. What matters is the infinite presence beyond the name, the Essence beyond the form we've attached to it.

Once we limit God to a belief system, we are bound to find others who share a different belief;

thus all the different religions. I'll never forget what Marianne Williamson said in her book *A Return to Love*: "Religion divides us, while spirituality unites us."

It is imperative that we get to a point where we understand that your belief doesn't take away from my belief, and vice versa. And that your religion and my religion point to the same infiniteness. What if we could say, "I honor your belief and you honor my belief"? It sounds so simple, yet it has baffled society for ages.

When people argue about one particular religion over another, I feel like saying, "What if love is our religion?" Most of the different religions tout love as the basic guiding premise. While each religion may use different terminology, have different stories or backgrounds, they are all really about the same deep underlying message: Love and connection.

I once had a conversation with a priest on an airplane. He described the different religions as spokes on a tire and God as the center hub. He said that there are many paths to God just as there are many spokes on the tire. One spoke may be Judaism, one may be Hinduism, one may be Islam, one may be Buddhism, one may be Christianity; but they all lead to the center hub: God.

I am reminded of a joke I heard one day about an atheist who was swimming in the ocean and suddenly found himself being circled by a shark. He just knew that he was going to be eaten by the shark. In his panic and desperation he yelled out to God, "Please save me!" Then God said, "Wait a minute. You're an atheist. I thought you didn't believe in me." The man remembered he was an atheist and said, "Good point." The shark continued circling him and approached him with open jaws. The man finally said, "I don't believe in you, but make the shark believe in you." Just as the shark was getting ready to chomp on the man, it stopped, backed away, and said, "Dear Lord, thank you for this meal, which I am about to receive."

I tell this funny story not to make fun of any particular belief but to illustrate our natural tendency to want others to conform to *our* beliefs. And what happens when we do this? We usually get eaten anyway, metaphorically.

A lot of people die and suffer when beliefs are imposed on others. I'd like to work on creating a world that honors all beliefs and accepts the fact that our mind-based beliefs all point to the same truth.

But how do we really honor someone else's belief? First it is important to remind ourselves that a belief is a construct of the mind.

But what if someone is coming at you with their beliefs? What do you do in this situation? How can you honor his or her belief?

Second, I learned the four most important words to say to someone when you have differing beliefs. Do you want to know what those four words are?

THANK YOU FOR SHARING

Those four words put an end to the arguments over differing beliefs. They allow others to express their beliefs and allow you to not have to defend or argue for yours.

If you sincerely say "Thank you for sharing," and then move on, you will have avoided an argument. What sense does it make to argue with others when you know that you will not change their beliefs and they will not change yours?

Just accept that everyone has different beliefs and that it doesn't make anyone right or wrong. And again, most religious beliefs, ultimately point to the same truth: Love.

The world is big enough for all kinds of beliefs. It's not about who's right or wrong but about moving beyond our differences and getting to that place where we can peacefully coexist.

Why spend our precious lives shooting rubber bands at one another?

Chapter 51
Us vs. Them

Different religious beliefs separate us, while honoring all beliefs unite us. When we don't honor other beliefs, it becomes an "us" versus "them" situation. Ultimately, there is no "us" and "them"; there is only "us," and we are all one.

When we were on the brink of the war in Iraq there was an appearance of separation. Every time you read the news or watched it on television, there was coverage of all these opposing forces. There were the peace activists, those who wanted us to support our troops, and those who supported war; and each group thought it was right.

We even saw and heard some peace activists making derogatory comments with a hateful energy toward our president and other political leaders, which seemed to be contradictory to the energy of peace.

Anytime you oppose something you are adding to the energy that created the problem in the first place.

What we've realized is that war and violence are often the result of having different viewpoints and not being able to reconcile them. And so by holding on to our viewpoints as being better than another's, we only add to the conflict.

For example, when people are outraged by the acts of the terrorists and feel justified in killing the terrorists, they are no different from the terrorists who feel justified in killing Americans.

When we use violence to impose our beliefs or authority over anyone, we are no better than the terrorists who use their anger and weapons because they feel justified that *we* are the bad guys.

In fact, most wars and acts of violence result from people declaring that they are right and that the wrong doers need to be persecuted.

When Einstein said that you "can't solve a problem from the same level of thinking that created the problem," he meant that by fighting fire with more fire, we all get burned.

The solution lies in moving beyond our apparent differences, our apparent need to prove how right we are and to make others suffer if they don't agree.

The solution is going to come from a change in consciousness. The solution will come when we realize that we are all connected.

At a core level, we all want the same thing. Ideally, we all want peace and we all want love. Most people wouldn't choose conflict, struggle, or violence. And if they do, they are often choosing conflict, struggle, or violence to defend a cause or their false sense of self.

Even the people who want to go to war want peace. Even the terrorists want peace. They want the peace that they believe will result after the war or the peace they believe will result after the effects of terrorism or after their way has been imposed. They all want the peace that they believe war or violence buys them.

If we move beyond these levels of apparent differences and know that at a core level we all want the same thing, that's when a shift will happen. If we realized our oneness with others, would we really try to harm them if we knew we were harming ourselves as well?

So how do we move beyond "us vs. them?" And how do we realize our connectedness? How do we manifest world peace?

The rest of part four will be devoted to ways we can realize our unity and thus create a peaceful earth.

Chapter 52

Transparency

Let's look at the bubble analogy again. What we love most about bubbles is their transparency. We can see right through them, which is part of their beauty.

Well, what if we could connect with each other as if we were transparent? What if I looked at you and didn't see what color you were, what clothes you wore, what actions you demonstrated, what beliefs you held. What if, instead, I could see right through you to the core level of your being?

What would the world be like if we all did that?

What if we could really connect with each other at a soul level, a level not based on judgment about such things as looks, beliefs, status, or actions?

We can connect with one another at this level, but it takes practice. It's a matter of developing your vision to see beyond the person—to see beyond his or her beliefs or actions. Remember the x-ray vision that cartoon superheroes had? Well, we can develop our transparency vision by connecting with people at a soul level.

The next time you look at someone, see beyond clothes and external appearance. See beyond their words or actions. Connect with his or her Essence. Pretend that you both are invisible—that you both are pure Spirits. Because that is the Truth.

The other day I had the opportunity to use this technique. Someone was talking to me and he was a little angry, not at me, but at a current situation.

All I could see was this angry person, complaining and moaning.

Yet I decided to use my transparent vision. I just looked at him deeply. Instead of seeing the anger, I was able to sense the transparency of the person—as if there was no separation between him and me, as if we were invisible. It was a surreal moment.

Without my saying anything, the person calmed down and then worked through his own thoughts and came to a positive conclusion on his own. I just stood there and said nothing.

Practicing this is like affirming the truth of others beyond their form. You're connecting with the truth of who they are beyond their looks or actions, and somehow in this presence, the truth of who they are is revealed.

Practice viewing people as transparent and connecting with them at that core level. Know that everyone is pure Spirit. See right through them to their Essence.

Chapter 53
Send Someone Love

Another way you can connect with others at the level of Essence and therefore transform your relationship is to send them love. Instead of snapping your rubber band at them, send a blessing of love their way.

A *Course in Miracles* says that everything is love or a call for love. So if something doesn't look or feel like love, then what is it? It's a call for love. And what do you do when people are calling for love? Give them love.

Here is a great meditation to practice if you're feeling separate. It's great for transforming any relationship in which there is conflict, tension, or hostility.

If you are having a conflict or strenuous relationship with anyone, whether it is a co-worker, family member, or public figure, *know* that the person is really only calling for love, and what do you do when someone is calling for love? You send love.

A powerful technique is to send someone love energetically through meditation. When you send love to someone you are in conflict with, the relationship will transform.

Meditation for Sending Love

During your prayers or meditations, picture the person in your mind's eye as vividly as possible. Or visualize the situation or experience you were involved in with the person.

Then picture that person surrounded by, bathed in, and supported in love.

You can do this many ways: You can picture physically giving love, by stroking his or her hair, by giving him or her a hug. Or you can picture love as a color that pours out from your heart and surrounds the person. The person would be bathed in this color, surrounded by this color. You can visualize sending love to this person in any way that seems appropriate for you.

Then take it a step further and see the person responding to that love. See him or her smiling and responding as a baby would when coddled by its mother.

See the person feeling absolutely loved, like an innocent child. See him or her feeling secure and peaceful. Repeat this meditation often until your relationship is transformed.

I guarantee that if you continue this meditation, your relationship with that person will be transformed. And that doesn't mean the person changes, though he or she may. It means that your relationship with that person (your reaction toward him or her) will change.

Send Someone Love

You can also do this with the planet. You can picture the earth surrounded and bathed in love, and then see all the earth's inhabitants exuding love.

I have created a wonderful series of guided meditations that will help you experience peace in your life, your relationships, and the world. For more information go to: *www.lessonsfromarubberband.com*

Chapter 54
Seek to Understand

Another way to transform our relationships with others and heal our sense of separation from them is to be able to understand their point of view.

A while back, I went to a weekend coaching seminar put on by my friends Renee and Anthony Choice. They led us in an exercise in which we paired up with another person and answered the question, "If you could be an animal, what animal would you be and why?" Then we were to share our answers.

I knew immediately that I would be a dolphin. I would be a dolphin because they're so playful, so free—so graceful. As I thought about a dolphin, I felt playful and limitless.

Then my partner said that if he could be an animal, he would be a spider. I gulped. My heart rate increased. I have an irrational fear of spiders. They are so creepy and crawly and scary looking. Yikes!

But then his eyes started to sparkle. He smiled and said, "I would be a spider because they create these magnificently beautiful webs. The webs are so delicate, so artistic, and so beautiful when they glisten in the sun. And if for some reason the web gets damaged, the spider just goes right into making another one. They are such fascinating creatures."

Suddenly, I saw spiders in a new light. Hmmm. I never thought about them that way before. I shared with him my fear of spiders and thanked him for giving me this new perspective. (Granted my irrational fear of spiders still comes back to me, but for that moment, I looked at spiders in a whole new light).

I would like to share a story with you about what it means to really understand someone else's point of view, and then I'll tell you how I used the example from the story to heal a relationship with my mother.

Angry Man in a Bus Station

It was Christmastime at a crowded bus station. People were dressed in their fine clothes, waiting to visit loved ones for the holiday. There were people carrying presents adorned with ribbons and bows of green and red. Everyone was smiling and singing. It was a festive moment.

One man stood out in the crowd. Why? Because he was rude and obnoxious. He had an angry face filled with hatred; you could see it in his eyes. His forehead was crinkled and he glared at anyone he made eye contact with.

The man reeked of body odor, and his physical appearance was disheveled. He wore mangled clothes, and his facial hair was matted together.

His language was obscene, and under his breath he was cursing at everyone. Not only that, but he was obscenely drunk. He teetered and stammered as he bumped into anyone in his path. He had no concern for the space of others.

Seek to Understand

People at the bus station were getting upset at the actions of this vile man. Many of them decided to push him back when he bumped into them.

One young man pushed the drunken man when he bumped into him, and said, "Watch where you're going, Jerk."

When the drunken man was pushed, he became easily off balance and bumped into more people. Everyone started pushing back and yelling things: "Jerk, Scumbag."

This only fueled the anger already in the man's heart. He cursed louder and became more obscene. Before you knew it, everyone in the bus station was full of anger and disgust.

Suddenly, one young man who couldn't take it any more took it upon himself to teach the old man a lesson. He pushed the drunken man so hard that he fell over and landed near a woman sitting on a bench with her eight-year-old daughter.

The eight-year-old girl looked at the man trying to get up, and then looked at her mom. "We should help him, don't you think?" she asked her mom.

The mother responded, "Normally, dear, we'd help, but not in this situation. This is different." The mother silently prayed that the vile man would not come over and disturb them.

Suddenly, the little girl got up and went over to the man, who had now stood up.

The little girl looked the man directly in the eyes and said, "Sir, why are you so angry?"

The drunken man slurred his words and yelled at the little girl to go away. "Leave me alone," he yelled.

The little girl was persistent. She pulled on his shirt and got the man's attention.

"Leave me alone. Get away from me," he said.

The little girl again looked him in the eyes and said, "The reason I asked is because I was wondering if there was anything I could do to help."

The man froze in his tracks. The angry look on his face softened, and he broke into tears.

The three of them, the drunken man, the little girl, and the mother, cried together.

They found out that a year ago, the drunken man's wife had died. They had been living paycheck to paycheck as it was, and with the high cost of funeral expenses and the downgrade to only one salary, the man took a turn for the worse. He lost his car and lost his home, and most importantly, he lost the love of his life. He became homeless.

On that day, the one-year anniversary of his wife's death, he had sold his only winter jacket in order to get bus fare so he could visit his wife at the cemetery.

Does knowing this information about the man help us understand his anger? Almost anyone in that same situation would experience anger.

Often we see only an outer act of anger and can't see the inner pain that's causing it. If we knew what was going on in a person's life, maybe we would have more empathy. I love this quote from Longfellow: "If we could read the secret history of our enemies, we should find in each person's life sorrow and suffering enough to disarm all hostility."

What if we knew that our angry co-worker was going through a devastating divorce? What if we knew that the angry stranger who just bumped into us at the grocery store had gone through a bankruptcy and lost everything? What if we knew that our angry boss had just buried his son? What if we knew that the angry woman at the cash register was being physically abused?

Would knowing that information soften our feelings toward people in those situations? Could we understand their anger?

It is helpful to remind ourselves that people who lash out in anger are acting from a place of deep pain. Wouldn't it be helpful to know what that pain is? And if it's not possible to know what the pain is, as in the case of strangers, wouldn't it be nice, instead of looking at them as angry people, to send healing prayers to them?

What if we sent prayers of love and support to them?

Put yourself in someone else's shoes. I think all miscommunication and misdirected hatred comes from lack of understanding where others are coming from.

A long time ago, my relationship with my mother wasn't very peaceful. I felt as if she was constantly nagging me (shooting the rubber band at me), and I would defend myself by saying, "I did this, I did that . . ." (shooting the rubber band back). And I'd end up completely stressed out after our conversations.

Then one day, after reading the peace prayer of St. Francis of Assisi with the verse "Seek not to be understood, but to understand," I tried to understand why my mom would nag me so much. I tried to put myself in her shoes. I asked myself, "If I were a mother, why would I nag my daughter?" My answer was, "Because I would want the very best for her. Because I love her so much." Then I realized how much my mother loved me and wanted the very best for me. So when I could really understand her side, I wasn't so defensive and instead felt grateful that she loved me so much. It has literally transformed our relationship.

But sometimes we can't understand the other person's point of view. Why is the cashier so rude? Why is that co-worker so obnoxious?

Sometimes we believe that there is absolutely no justification for others' actions. In these cases, I like to play the "What if?" game. What if I found out that the cashier had just lost her son, or what if I knew that my co-worker was going through a devastating divorce? Would I treat them differently? Would I be able to not take their actions personally and instead let them just bounce right off of me? I probably would, if I knew they were hurting in some way. I wouldn't take things so personally.

Seek to Understand

Sometimes we don't know why people behave in certain ways. But one thing is for sure: if they are acting out in anger, they have deep pain underneath. Maybe if we tried to understand their pain or empathize with their pain, we could keep from getting shot with their rubber bands and keep from shooting them with our rubber bands.

And as I said earlier, I also think a large part of understanding has to do with knowing the background, values, religious beliefs, and culture of others. I think understanding others helps us honor our connection with them.

I have created a program called International Pen Pals that involves carrying on discussions with people from all over the world to better understand their lives. Understanding is a necessary step toward love and peace.

For more information, go to our Web site at: *www.peacefulearth.com/forum*. Then click on the topic International, and then on International Peace Pen Pals.

Chapter 55
Victims and Perpetrators

What about perpetrators of crime? How can we understand their point of view? Why should we even try?

Studies have shown that many perpetrators of crime were at one time victims of crime themselves. This is especially true in cases of child abuse. Often, perpetrators of acts of violence against children were abused as children. That is why many programs are aimed at "breaking the cycle" of violence.

How do we really break the cycle of violence? Our society has become good at locking people up. I have to wonder if this solves the problem as violence has been, and continues to be, on the increase every year.

In the news, we sometimes hear about the living conditions, the emotional state, or the past of criminals who commit violent crimes. I am struck by amazing similarities every time I hear about the inner lives of most criminals. Most often, the following conditions describes them in some way—many of them were poor and lived in terrible conditions most of their lives, suffering from abuse and neglect on a regular basis. Many of them were outcasts most of their lives. Many of them were addicted to drugs, alcohol or sex, and most of them had never known a loving relationship or had a positive role model. I know there are always exceptions to everything. I have heard of a case where a person who seemingly had everything, committed an unspeakable crime. For the most part, the patterns and circumstances are the same. The perpetrator was in deep pain and had no other way to express it. He became "unconscious".

I use the term "unconscious" here to mean that their Imposter has taken over (chapter 14). At this point, they have forgotten who they really are—an expression of God.

So, doesn't it seem that a great part of reducing acts of violence would be to remind people of who they really are; to show them love and to remind them that we are all connected?

I recently watched a show on Public Broadcast by Wayne Dyer. He was promoting his new book, *Inspiration*. On the show, he talked about how a tribe in South Africa punishes people accused of violent behavior or crime by putting the person on trial in the center of the group and have everyone circle around him/her. Then, they go around the circle and everyone says positive things about the person on trial. They say what they like about him/her; what they feel are his/her best attributes, etc. They only say positive, uplifting things. Ironically, this tribe in South Africa rarely even has to use this system!

Can you put yourself in a perpetrator's shoes and imagine how overwhelmed you'd be if everyone was telling you how loved you are—how you are forgiven and how nothing you do can tarnish who you really are?

Victims and Perpetrators

I really believe that everything is love or a call for love, and that people who commit crimes are really calling for love in the only way they know how. Yes, the crying out is often insane and should not be condoned, but what if the perpetrators really felt loved, felt listened to, and felt like they were cared about? Would we have as much crime or violence in our world? My guess would be that we wouldn't.

What if the principles in this book and others, could be taught to troubled juveniles, gang members, and prisoners? What if these teens felt loved? Would it make a difference? I believe it would.

The other powerful thing about the Public Broadcast program with Wayne Dyers, was that he had a guest on the program, a lady from Rwanda, that survived genocide. She hid in a 3X4 closet, with seven other women, to avoid being killed. The women hid in that box for three months, and could not speak, shower or barely move!

The amazing thing was that she talked about the importance of forgiveness. She said that she forgives the perpetrators of that massive genocide. If she can forgive, can't we?

Jesus' statement, "Forgive them, they know not what they do" is such a powerful example. Again, I believe that perpetrators like this are in so much pain that they are literally "unconscious" and that they really don't know what they are doing. How do we solve this "unconsciousness"? By being unconscious as well? No, we shine the light of our consciousness into every situation! We respond with love. They too, are calling for love, even though it is in an insane way. Our responsibility is to work on forgiveness.

The woman from Rwanda also talked about how, if these militia men would have known these spiritual principles; that they are one with God, and that we are all connected, they would not have committed such crimes against innocent people, including their own.

I've struggled with this issue too. How can I forgive someone like those militia men who kill innocent children? All that I know is to turn within and forgive.

If people knew they were whole and complete and pure, perfect love, would things be this way? If people knew that, if I hurt you, I only hurt myself. Would we have as much violence?

After watching the Public Broadcast program I felt compelled to write a letter to a prisoner, incarcerated for any crime, as part of a healing process.

What if you were a prisoner who committed an act of crime from a place of pain? How would you feel if you received a letter like this? And, do parts of this letter seem like something God would say to us about forgiveness?

Letter to a Prisoner

Dear Friend,

I don't know you by name, and I don't know what crime you've committed. I don't know about your past, or your specific situation.

All I know is that whatever you did in the past can't take away from the Truth of who you really are.

You are whole and perfect in every way. You are pure love. If you at any time weren't expressing pure love, then you temporarily forgot who you were. You were probably calling out for love in the only way you knew how.

You most likely haven't had any role models to love you and guide you along the way. You may have even felt abandoned by society.

You've probably seen and experienced things that most of us have never seen.

You were most likely acting from fear or anger. But, you are more than your past, your pain or your situation.

You are not your past. You are not your circumstances. You are not what happened to you or even what you did. You are pure Spirit.

I am deeply sorry for whatever you have experienced that has made you lash out in any way. I am sorry for any pain you have endured. I know that you have done the best with the knowledge you had at the time.

Know that you are completely forgiven for anything that you have done that may have caused others to suffer.

Really, when hurting others, you are only hurting yourself. Others serve as mirrors for the way you feel about yourself. At the most basic level, we are all connected, we are all one.

In this moment, all your past is gone. The past is only alive in your memory.

Now you have a choice. You can remember that you are pure Spirit. You can forgive yourself, and allow that love to shine through. There is no problem too great that cannot be healed by love.

And love is who you are, and absolutely nothing that you've done, can erase that truth.

Chapter 56
"FORE"giveness

Another way to transform relationships is through forgiveness. The reason this topic is in part four about how to stop hurting others with our rubber bands is because most of us think that when we forgive others, we indeed stop shooting them with our rubber bands. But the fact is that when we forgive others, we really stop hurting ourselves.

Really, when we practice forgiveness we free ourselves and we transform our relationships and ultimately, the world.

I had an epiphany about forgiveness one day on a golf course.

There I was on a sunny afternoon on a beautiful golf course in Northern California—the rolling greens, the redwoods, and the crisp air were exactly what I had needed.

I had just walked away from a clearly one-sided relationship in which I was ready for a commitment, and my partner wasn't. We had been off and on for over a year, and I had tried and tried. He was younger than I, and he wasn't interested in a commitment. The only thing he was committed to was snowboarding and partying.

Anyway, we had just broken up and I was angry. I was angry with myself for releasing my heart to the care of someone who didn't want it. I was angry with him for not being ready for a commitment. I oscillated between blaming myself and blaming him for the demise of the relationship. Neither scenario made me feel any better.

I needed to get away, to not think about the relationship; so I decided to go golfing. I knew it would soothe my soul. The calmness and quietness of the outdoors, the beautiful landscape, and the meditative concentration required by the sport would serve as my escape from reality.

I remember teeing off. I focused my entire concentration on the ball and visualized exactly where I wanted it to land. I was at that place of complete focus when all of a sudden a loud yell broke my concentration. A nearby golfer yelled, "Fore . . ."

I covered my head, while cautiously looking for the flying golf ball. It miraculously landed about ten feet away from me, leaving me unharmed.

Then it hit me. Not the golf ball, but the parallels between my golf experience and my relationships.

I realized that because I was a golfer, I knew that "fore" meant to "beware of a flying golf ball;" therefore my behavior was appropriate.

But I also remembered that the first time I was out on the golf course, I had no idea what the word "fore" meant. At that time, if someone had yelled fore, I would have just stood there, an open target for a soaring golf ball.

That's when I realized that most mistakes or accidents occur because of our innocence—from not knowing the rules of the game. And that when we're playing in unfamiliar territory, our behavior matches our skill level. Our results, whether it is a broken heart or a welt on the head from a flying golf ball, depend on our familiarity with the game of love or of golf.

At the time of my relationship with that younger man, I didn't know any better. I just knew I had feelings for him, and I acted on them. He didn't know any better either. He was young and unsure of what he wanted out of life. We both behaved innocently. We both just didn't know the rules of the game completely.

I found it much easier to forgive myself, to stop berating myself, once I realized that I did the best I could, and that I just didn't know all the rules of the game of love. Just like at one time I didn't know the rules of golf.

I also felt better looking at him as an innocent bystander who got hit by a golf ball because he didn't know the rules of the game.

It occurred to me that we all are doing our best with the knowledge that we have at the time.

To me, this is what forgiveness is: realizing our innocence, affirming the other person's innocence, and then moving on.

Forgiveness really is a gift we give to ourselves. I've heard it said that *not* forgiving someone is like "drinking poison and expecting someone else to die." Not forgiving someone is like having a poison circulating through your bloodstream. It affects you, and not the other person.

Forgiveness is a way of loving ourselves and loving the other person. People often ask whether forgiveness means that you're condoning the act.

No, forgiveness doesn't mean that you condone the act, only that you release it. It's not about labeling the act as right or wrong but about realizing that we all do the best we can with the knowledge we have at the time. Forgiveness is about releasing.

People often ask whether forgiveness means that you should stay with the person who harmed you. No, you should not be with someone who harms you physically or jeopardizes your safety. You can lovingly release a person through forgiveness, but that doesn't mean you have to stay with him or her, unless you choose to do so.

Another common question people ask is how they will know when they have forgiven someone. You have forgiven someone completely when you can think of that person or run into that person and not have any reaction.

If you are still feeling animosity, pressure, stress, anger, or tension, that means you need to do more forgiveness work. When you can see or think of the person and not have any adverse reaction, then you have forgiven.

Again, my way to forgive others is to acknowledge that they did the best they knew how to do at the time. Plain and simple.

We may not know or understand why someone did a particular act, and often we are not meant to know or to figure it out. There can be many reasons, such as past programming, an abusive childhood, or lack of self esteem. The reasons do not matter. The grace to forgive and to love others unconditionally, in spite of what they did—that is what matters.

Chapter 57
Grudges

Many of us hold grudges against other people for what they did. But if you think about it, grudges are really about the people who hold them—and their need to be right. A grudge is a need to be right at all costs.

I put the topic of grudges in this part of the book because most of us would think of holding grudges as hitting others with our rubber bands. As with forgiveness, when we hold a grudge we are really snapping ourselves with our rubber bands.

I know about grudges well. I held a grudge against my dad for quite a while. It all started when my husband and I were planning our wedding.

We were planning a small, intimate ceremony in Hawaii and wanted to incorporate our family. Both of my parents and stepparents live out of town, so I called and left messages with them about our Hawaii plan and asked them how involved they wanted to be and what dates they were available.

I heard back from my mom and my prospective in-laws immediately. But I didn't hear back from my dad. He had informed me a few weeks earlier that he and my stepmother *might* be out of the country around the time of our planned wedding date, but I hadn't heard any final details. I sent an E-mail and left another message.

We didn't hear back from him for a week, so we proceeded with our plans. We had to book the airfare, the hotel, and the wedding planner. Sure enough, the day after we booked our wedding and honeymoon, my dad called and said that their three-week trip out of the country started on the exact date of our wedding.

Unfortunately, we purchased nonrefundable tickets, and everyone else had already made their plans. Anyway, my stepmother got on the phone with my dad and me, and a big argument ensued. The basic tune was that I was spoiled, that I didn't even take my father into consideration, and that I had put him through a rough time.

After a few words were said, I hung up. I didn't speak to my dad for a long time and continued with our wedding plans. I was angry. I held a deep grudge toward my dad and stepmother. In my mind, it was their fault for not calling me back, not taking us seriously, and not being more involved.

And in my father's mind, I was not very accommodating to his schedule, and it probably felt to him that I wasn't really taking them into consideration.

Anyway, I still held a grudge. I was hurting inside. I wanted to share our wedding plans with my dad, I wanted to have a relationship with him, but I was too proud. I was holding a grudge.

That's when I realized that a grudge is really the need to be right. The reason I was holding a grudge was because I thought I was right and he was wrong.

Therefore, I felt I should not call him. I felt justified in my anger.

But then I remembered a quote from *A Course in Miracles*: "Would you rather be right or happy?"

I thought about how children who play together may feud, but the next minute they are playing together again. They forget their need to be right because playing is more fun.

Holding this grudge wasn't helping me. It wasn't making me happy. And it wasn't doing anything for our relationship.

Finally, my dad and I talked. We all decided to have a reception in Oregon after our wedding, and my dad and stepmother would come up for that. It all worked out beautifully.

But I had to release my need to be right. How did being right serve me?

So if you're holding a grudge toward someone, ask yourself if it's because of your need to be right. If the answer is yes, ask, "How does being right serve you?"

Often, our need to be right makes us sacrifice relationships with those we love. Instead of worrying about who is right or wrong, we need to shift our focus to "Why does it even matter who is right or wrong?"

I could go to my grave being right, and where would that get me?

Surrender the need to be right. Realize that in the big scheme of things, it doesn't matter. Would you rather be right or have a loving relationship?

Chapter 58
Listening as a Loving Act

Another way we can transform our relationships with our family, friends, co-workers, and others is by really listening to them.

Not listening to others is equivalent to shooting them with our rubber bands.

I remember reading a statistic that said most perpetrators of violent crimes committed them because they hadn't felt heard. They had tried to get someone's attention, and it didn't work; so in desperation, they resorted to violent actions to make themselves heard.

Domestic disputes often arise because one or both of the parties don't feel heard. Often one party then resorts to acts (throwing, hitting) that draw attention or make the other person listen.

Well, what would happen if we listened more? Could that in any way reduce the amount of violence? Is listening a way to love someone?

Remember a time when you were upset about something and you shared your feelings with a friend or a partner and afterward you felt so much better? Why? Because you were listened to. Listening to someone really is a great act of love.

On the next page is a technique for truly listening to another person.

Active Listening Technique

When people talk to you . . .

* Make sure that you make eye contact with them.

* Fully listen to what they are saying by not interrupting.

* When they are finished, repeat back to them, in your own words, what you heard them say.

This technique produces amazing results. I have used it as an exercise in many of my "Playshops" (I call them "playshops" because they are much too fun to be workshops) and people always say that they really felt loved and supported and *heard* when this technique was used.

So, when another person is talking, instead of thinking about the next thing you're going to say, or how you are going to make your point, take the time to fully listen to what the other person is saying.

Chapter 59
Acknowledging Others

One of the simplest ways we can maintain loving relationships and even create peace is to acknowledge people for who they are.

When the book *Peaceful Earth* came out I created some Peace Prizes as well. They were small laminated cards given to people who were seen demonstrating kind or loving acts. They were a way to acknowledge people for their kindness. And they were also a way to encourage continued acts of kindness. Often, when we are acknowledged for a simple gesture, we will do more of those gestures.

Moreover, I realized that the Peace Prizes became a great tool to help people focus on peaceful loving acts, thus creating a more peaceful reality (more about this in the chapter "See Peace").

Saying thank you to others has such a wonderful effect on them, on you, and on the world. You can say thank you through an E-mail, a card, or a verbal acknowledgment.

I got in the habit of sending thank-you cards to the coordinators who would book my speaking engagements and book signings. I heard back from several of them, thanking me for thanking them. Most of them said that they were never thanked for all the work they do to organize events.

I also make it a habit of thanking my husband, family, and friends. Often, I don't thank them for specific things they did, but just for being a part of my life.

I invite you to think of five people you would like to thank for something. Then verbally express your gratitude, or send them a card or E-mail. Make it a habit of giving thanks and acknowledging others.

You can send someone a free Peace Prize or a free E-card from our Web site at *www.peacefulearth.com* under Peaceful Relationships.

Let people know how special they are. The amazing thing is that it makes you feel good and grateful for having such wonderful people in your life.

A little acknowledgment goes a long way. Giving thanks and acknowledgment to others for who they are and for the little acts of kindness they do is a critical key to manifesting a peaceful earth.

Chapter 60
Cooperation Instead of Competition

I have developed a supportive relationship with a woman who is a spiritual author. We have never met, but we have E-mailed back and forth, and I am familiar with her books and mission as she is familiar with mine.

She was working on a campaign to bring one of her recent books to the top of Amazon's best-seller list. As part of the appeal to buy the book, many bonus items were offered. We talked about including my peace E-course as one of the bonus items. The E-course would be free to anyone who took advantage of her offer. The woman had quite an impressive list of free products that were available if you purchased her book. I also agreed to send out an announcement of her offer to my subscriber list.

A couple of weeks before the announcement was supposed to be sent out, I had second thoughts: "If I send out this offer to my list, people will purchase her book and get my E-course for free. What will I get out of it?" I would be selling and promoting her product, and I would not get any financial gain from it. Furthermore, if I later decided to send out an offer on one of my products, people might not be as willing to buy my stuff since they had just purchased something else. On and on, my mind went. I kept wondering why I was helping her sell her product and if doing so would be decreasing sales for my own products. This battle went on in my mind for some time.

I also know that in the past, when I have asked others to help me spread the message about some of my products, they have not agreed to do so. Yet the next week these same people would turn around and promote a "friend's" product or one of their own products.

I realized that part of the problem is similar to the "us vs. them" mentality, but instead it is my product vs. your product. If I help you promote your product, then my product may not sell. Or I choose to promote my product instead of your product.

What if the "my" and the "your" were dropped? What if we looked at all of the products as products that will benefit a lot of people regardless of the creator? Or what if I realized that by promoting your product, I was offering a service to people? What if I knew that promoting your product wouldn't take away from my product?

Part of this competition revolves around the belief that there isn't enough to go around and that if I help you, somehow there will be less available for me. This is a limiting belief. The Universe is infinite. There is more than enough for everyone.

It is the spirit of cooperation instead of competition that will ultimately benefit *all* of us. Think of it this way: If you go to a movie and really love it and recommend it to your friends, do you feel as if you just let them in on a secret and that telling them about the movie has taken away your experience of the movie? No, of course not. You tell your friends and family about a good movie because you want them to share in that experience. That same idea should apply to everything.

What if I'm a musician and I hear a good piece of music? If I told someone about a certain CD, would that diminish sales of my CD? Or, as an author, if I read a good book and recommend it, does that limit the sales of my book?

I constantly recommend Eckhart Tolle's book the *Power of Now* because it has made a real impact on my life. I am not afraid that by doing so, my book will be less well received. Yet I was feeling a sense of competition when I offered to send out this other announcement to my list.

So in this situation I found an opportunity—an opportunity to foster a sense of cooperation instead of competition. I sent out the announcement to my list knowing that I was recommending something that could really affect their life positively. And if that woman's book goes on to be a top-selling book on Amazon, hurray! We all joined together to accomplish it.

At the time of this writing, this woman has also agreed to help me spread the message of this book in any way she can.

There is an opportunity here for you as well: Any time you feel in competition with someone—help them succeed. Do whatever you can to support them, to help them win, or to help them get ahead. Instead of competition, practice cooperation.

The spirit of cooperation sends a strong message to the Universe that you are willing to work with others for the greatest good of everyone and that there is plenty for everyone. And ultimately the Universe will respond by recruiting others to help you in that same spirit of cooperation.

Chapter 61
Our Effect on Others

Part of realizing world peace is to acknowledge our effect on others.

We've all heard the quote from Gandhi: "The pure love of one person can offset the hatred of thousands." What a powerful illustration of the power of love. It has now begun to be proven scientifically and medically that a person's presence has an energetic effect on others.

People often ask whether, by showing up as peace and love, we can really have an effect on others and on the world. Many people have a hard time believing that just their presence can affect change. Many wonder how their small acts could even make a difference.

A good book to read if you question the effect we have on others is *Power vs. Force* by David R. Hawkins, M.D., Ph.D. In the book, he scientifically demonstrates the effect that one person has on others. He mentions that an Avatar at a high level of consciousness "can, in fact, totally counterbalance the collective negativity of all mankind." For a full explanation of levels of consciousness, see Hawkins' book.

In 1960, Maharishi predicted that one percent of a population practicing the Transcendental Meditation technique would produce measurable improvements in the quality of life for the whole population. The

Maharishi Effect has proven that, through focused prayer and meditation, a reduction in violent crimes occurs.

But we don't have to understand the scientific studies to understand our effect on others because we witness it in our daily lives.

For example, have you ever noticed that after being around a co-worker who was stressed, high strung, and rude, you yourself felt stressed and in high gear? What about the opposite? Have you ever been around someone who was so bubbly and such fun to be with, and when you left, you yourself were smiling and nice to others?

These are practical examples of our effect on others.

So, if we have an effect on others and if it has been documented and if we have witnessed it in our daily lives, the question becomes, what effect do we choose to have on others?

Do we want to brighten the room? Or do we want to agitate people because of our negativity?

Through being peaceful, we have a peaceful effect on others. It has been said that Jesus could heal people from his mere presence. Further, the Bible says that we shall do these things and even greater.

First, we must own the truth that our energy does affect those around us. Then we must choose which energy we bring into the world.

Our Effect on Others

And we must never doubt what Gandhi said, "That the pure love of one person can offset the hatred of thousands."

We must use our individual energetic power wisely to create the type of world we want to see.

Chapter 62
See Peace

Another simple, but profound, way to manifest peace is to see peace. When we shoot rubber bands out, we most likely get them shot back at us. When we exude peace, we get peace back.

The story below illustrates how what we see becomes our reality.

There was a building that had a huge hall of mirrors. The hall was completely covered with mirrors. There were mirrors everywhere—on the floor, the ceiling, and the sides.

One day a dog walks into the hall of mirrors and sees himself surrounded by all of these other dogs. He immediately gets defensive and starts snarling. Of course, all of the other dogs get defensive and start snarling back. Then of course the dog gets really angry and starts snarling even more aggressively and starts salivating and looking really mean.

Then all the other dogs start snarling and salivating as well. They look ferocious. The dog eventually rolls over and dies of exhaustion trying to defend itself against all of the other mean-looking dogs.

A few days later another dog walks into that same hall of mirrors. He sees himself surrounded by all these other dogs that—he could *play* with. He immediately gets happy and starts wagging his tail. Of course all the other dogs get happy and start wagging their tails. This dog rolls over in complete joy from being surrounded by so many playful companions.

Same hall of mirrors but a different experience for each dog. What each dog chose to see became its reality. Can this be true?

There are many books on the subject of perception and reality, and I encourage anyone interested to explore this topic in more detail. A wonderful book to read is *The Spontaneous Fulfillment of Desire* by Deepak Chopra.

In this book, Dr. Chopra reveals a concept in quantum physics that involves the phenomenon of the observer and the observed. To put it simply, it says that the object being viewed changes, depending on the stance or situation of the viewer.

Experiments have been done in which a particle has been isolated; and at certain times upon viewing it, the particle appeared as a wave, and at other times it appeared as a particle.

The same theories apply in medicine. Often what we see becomes our experience. In college, one of my favorite courses was immunology. I wrote a paper on the mind-body connection. One experiment I will never forget was about the power of thought.

The power of thought has long been recognized as an important connection in the healing and disease process, and there are literally hundreds of articles and books to read about the subject. But this one particular experiment always stood out in my mind.

A group of patients had been diagnosed with cancer. The doctors gave all the patients chemotherapy to cure their cancer. All of the patients were told that the chemotherapy would make their hair fall out.

Amazingly, half of the patients were given a placebo (a sugar pill) instead of the chemotherapy, and yet their hair still fell out. They had been told that their hair would fall out from the medication, and they believed it; and sure enough it did fall out, even though they didn't take any chemical that would make their hair fall out.

Again, there are hundreds of studies out there about this phenomenon: whatever we see or believe becomes our reality.

When I worked at a hospital full time, it seemed that every time a co-worker was sick, I ended up getting sick too. If an employee was coughing or sneezing around me, I'd say, "Oh great, now I'm going to get sick," and sure enough I would.

There are probably hundreds of small examples that happen every day that prove to us the power our thoughts have on our reality. Have you ever been heading to an important meeting and thought to yourself, "Oh great, I'm going to be late," and then you were late?

Or on the flip side, have you ever found yourself in traffic and thought to yourself, "It'll be okay, I'll still get there," and amazingly you got to your meeting on time? I'm sure we all can think of some major examples and some minor ones that illustrate the power of thought influencing our reality.

First, know that you have an effect on others. Second, notice when you have a limiting thought. Then start replacing limiting thoughts with affirmations.

Consciously look for peaceful people. You'll see them everywhere. Go to the Web site *www.peacefulearth.com* and get some Peace Prizes and focus on giving them to people who are peaceful and kind. This encourages us to actively look for peace.

If you develop your capacity to see love, peace, and joy all around you, these things will become your reality. Recognize what an awesome creator of the Universe you are.

Your Contribution to the World

Through all the lessons I've learned over the last five years of trying to make things happen, I have come to realize that the most significant factor in having a positive effect on the world, is our being, not our making or doing.

And while there are things that I do I always focus on doing from a place of being.

Really, our most significant contribution to the world comes from who we are, not from what we do. This reminds me of a billboard I once saw that said, "Who you are speaks so loudly, I can't hear what you're saying!"

As I mentioned earlier, I read a biography of Mother Teresa, who in terms of making things happen was very successful. She established and set up missionaries all over the world. Yet she herself said that often there were times when she couldn't do anything except be there for someone. She said that she felt her greatest contribution was listening to someone who was broken hearted, or touching the hand of someone who was sick.

For the longest time, I tried to make this book happen by trying to force myself to finish it. I wasn't making any progress. But when I sat back and meditated about what I wanted to say, the book just flowed, and I finished it rather quickly.

I now choose to focus on being, and living from the inside out; and I have to say that I am now experiencing more abundance and more fulfillment then I was when I was busy trying to *make* a difference in the world.

And while I continue to set goals and move forward with my writing, I enjoy being in the process. I take time out of my schedule to enjoy just being. I enjoy fully whatever it is I am doing. And if I get in a fear or worry space, I bring my focus back to doing what I do best by being my true self.

It seems that it is more pertinent to ask people how they are *being* instead of asking how they are doing. How are you living each moment to the fullest?

Mother Teresa was quoted as saying, "I'm just the pencil; God is the instrument." That illustrates a fluidity and a sense of just going with the flow.

As a writer, I know that when I try to force the words on paper, they don't come or they don't make sense; yet when I'm in the "God groove," things just flow and the words literally pour out.

So instead of cutting off the flow of life with our rubber bands, let's allow life to flow through us. And instead of denying our situations or shoving our rubber bands under the carpet, let's learn to accept them as they are.

And instead of judging ourselves, belittling ourselves, and hurting ourselves with our rubber bands, let's love and accept ourselves for the wonderful beings we are.

Your Contribution

If we as individuals remembered our connection with our Creator and lived from that place of connection, we would never experience fear, failure, lack, or stress. If we truly lived from the inside out we would experience inner peace, harmony, abundance, and love no matter what was going on in our lives.

And instead of hurting others with our anger, our beliefs, our judgments, let's put down our rubber bands and remember that we are all connected.

If we as individuals lived from that place of recognizing our unity and connection with others, we would experience peaceful and harmonious relationships as well as a peaceful earth.

This is the world I choose to manifest. Will you join me in remembering your true self and honoring your connection with others?

What's Next?

So here you are at the end of the book. Now what?

I invite you to take the rubber band challenge. Wear a rubber band around your wrist for at least a week. (Or you can order our rubber band bracelets from our Web site at: *www.lessonsfromarubberband.com*.)

Let the rubber band serve as a tool and a reminder of the lessons in this book.

Any time you try to make something happen, know that you are metaphorically twisting that rubber band around your wrist and cutting off the flow of life.

Any time you try to avoid or ignore your current situation, know that you will end up with a huge mess of rubber bands all tangled together that is difficult to clean up.

And any time you judge, worry, stress out, live in your past or become fearful, know that you are snapping yourself with your rubber band—you are literally hurting yourself.

And remember that any time you judge others, argue with them, don't listen to them, or are unwilling to understand their point of view, what you are doing is hurting them with your rubber band.

Teach these principles to others. Using the rubber band analogy is an easy way to teach people principles for living a peaceful, harmonious, joyous life.

Recommend this book to others. Help spread the message regarding these spiritual principles.

Also remember that 10% of the profits from this book go to organizations that help decrease human suffering on our planet. (Go to the Web site at *www.lessonsfromarubberband.com* to see which organizations this book currently supports).

But most of all, practice living from the inside out through meditation and affirmation and bask in the beauty of who you are and your unique contribution to the world.

Acknowledgments

I thank God every day for the gift of life.

I also did not get to where I am today without the support, love, and encouragement from others.

My deepest gratitude goes to my husband, Michael, who I believe was brought into my life as a direct result of my releasing that which didn't serve me and opening up to accept a truly loving, supportive relationship. Michael, thank you for encouraging me to show up as who I really am, and for supporting me on my journey. And thank you for inspiring me with your creativity and passion. Not a day goes by that I don't give thanks for the beauty, joy, and love we share.

Thank you to my mom (Jane) and dad (Paul) and my brother Paul. I absolutely know that I would not be where I am today without your support.

Thank you to my extended family: My step-parents Jay and Anna, and my in-laws, Bill and Kay who treat me as their own daughter.

Thank you to my dear friends: Lynda Mueller, Eric & Julianna Montgomery, Anthony & Renee Choice and Karen Foster, for being examples of pure Spirit, love, and talent. Thank you for your support, love, and encouragement.

And thank you Mike Gerdes for believing in me when no one else would even listen to me. Thank you for seeing more in me than I saw in myself. Thank you for encouraging me to follow my own inner voice and to realize that I had something worth saying.

#176 purpose
#190 qu-ph-
replication

About the Author

Lisa Hepner is the author/compiler of *Peaceful Earth: Spiritual Perspectives on Inner Peace and World Peace.*

Hepner is the founder and creator of the internationally recognized Web site Peaceful Earth (listed below).

Hepner has created numerous products and resources to support people in creating peace in their lives, their relationships and the world.

Her articles have been published in dozens of publications both online and in print.

Hepner received the 2006 Religious Science International Peace Award for her commitment and dedication to peace.

Hepner has dedicated her life to helping others express their truth and realize their connectedness.

Hepner engages audiences nationally with her dynamic story-telling.

You can contact Hepner through her Web sites at:

www.lessonsfromarubberband.com
www.peacefulearth.com
www.lisahepner.com

*You may also want to check out the following site in progress: www.bookswithamission.com.

Ordering Information

If you enjoyed this message, please help us spread the word. 10% of the profits of this book will be donated to organizations that help reduce suffering on the planet. (Go to the Web site to see which organizations this book currently supports).

Go to our Web site below to purchase any of our products.

If you haven't already, you may want to purchase a rubber band bracelet which will serve as a reminder of these principles. It's also a wonderful tool to use to explain these principles to others.

We also have meditations available for purchase. We will continually be updating our site to create more products that help you experience peace in your life, your relationships and the world.

Web sites:
www.lessonsfromarubberband.com
www.peacefulearth.com
www.bookswithamission.com

Mailing address:
Peaceful Earth, LLC
14845 SW Murray Scholls
Ste. 110, #302
Beaverton, OR 97007